First Edition 1996

Published by

BETROCK
INFORMATION SYSTEMS

7770 Davie Road Extension
Hollywood, Florida 33024-2516

Printed in the United States of America.

Library of Congress Catalog Card Number 96-84317
ISBN# 0-9629761-4-8

Graphic Design by Lissie Allen

CONTENTS

KUDOS

My special gratitude goes to those who took time to read this manuscript and to offer comments and criticism, based on their own expert knowledge. Although the final responsibility for the accuracy and validity of·the text is mine, I could not have completed this book without the generous help from the following persons: Alan W. Meerow, Ph.D., Associate Professor of Tropical Horticulture at the University of Florida and our editors at Betrock Information Systems, Inc., Donna Kurtzer, Kay Galletta and Linda Thorne. Also, I must acknowledge Irv Betrock, Publisher, for without his vision, this book would never have come to fruition.

Edward F. Gilman

INTRODUCTION

Gardening in Florida can be fun and rewarding when just a few simple principles are followed. When you combine common sense with the plant information provided in this guide, you can create a garden that requires less maintenance and looks fabulous. Be sure to spend a few moments browsing the introduction before reading the plant information. This will acquaint you with the simple gardening principles that will save you time and help you garden in an environmentally friendly manner.

This book describes a number of the more commonly available plants for landscaping in Florida. It is not intended to provide an exhaustive listing of all plants suited for Florida's diverse landscapes and climates. Most can be purchased at local nurseries, whereas others are harder to find. As the interest in plants continues to grow, nurseries will offer an increasingly wider selection of plants. Nursery operators are beginning to name and test cultivars selected from native populations. Others are introducing and testing non-native cultivars for their suitability here. Cultivars often exhibit an unusual or consistent attribute such as flower or fruit color, or canopy shape or size. Ask for a specific plant, such as a cultivar, at the nursery if you do not see it. They may be able to obtain it from a special source. If enough people ask for certain plants, more will become available. All plants and grasses in this book are listed alphabetically by scientific name, followed by the most widely used common name(s).

Choosing plants

Have you ever wondered why your neighbor's garden looks better than yours? The difference may lie in the fact that they performed a brief site analysis before making a trip to the garden center. Most successful gardeners understand the soil and light conditions in their landscapes and are aware that these have an important impact on plant performance. Before you go shopping for plants at the local garden center, consider your existing landscape conditions. Important attributes of the landscape that affect plant selection include minimum winter temperature, light exposure, pH, drainage, salt exposure and your personal preferences. Recent surveys by the University of Florida show that most people do not consider these before selecting plants. Many planting schemes fail because these points are improperly evaluated or even ignored.

After you consider the cultural attributes at the planting site, you can choose plants for their pretty flowers or other desirable characteristics.

Cold hardiness

Plants are adapted to regions of the state designated by hardiness zones (see map). The hardiness zone map was developed by the United States Department of Agriculture and was modified for this book to best coincide with Florida climatic conditions. The map specifies the lowest average winter temperature expected in a region. It is a fairly reliable guide in this respect, although there may be some winters with temperatures below normal. These temperatures could damage or kill plants designated as hardy in your area.

Each plant is given a hardiness zone range which indicates the most northern and most southern regions of the state for which the plant is adapted. The southern limit is given as a guide to how far south the plant can be used reliably. A plant grows less vigorously if located at the extreme northern or extreme southern edge of its recommended range.

Light exposure

Note how many hours of direct sun the planting site receives in the summer. Remember to account for the seasonal change in the sun angle when evaluating sites in other seasons. Plants requiring full sun, such as junipers, grow best with at least six hours of direct sun, but all-day sun often produces the best form and growth. Those suited for partial sun/partial shade will be adapted to a site receiving three or four hours of direct sun. Shade loving plants are adapted to sites with filtered sun or filtered shade, or those receiving less than two hours of direct sun (see Appendix 1, p.155).

Wind

Wind increases the amount of water lost from a plant to the atmosphere. Although well-managed irrigation can overcome some of this water deficit, the best method of managing water loss in a windy site is by proper species selection. Species tolerant of drought usually grow best in windy areas, unless soil is poorly drained. For these poorly-drained, windy sites, species that tolerate both wet soil and drought are best suited (see Appendix 4, p.157).

Salt

Airborne salt can affect plants through the twigs and foliage, or through roots after it is deposited on the ground. Plants within a quarter mile of the coastline, especially along the Atlantic Ocean, should possess some degree of tolerance to aerosol salt spray (see Appendix 2, p.156). Those exposed to direct spray along the dunes should be highly salt tolerant. Salt tolerant plants such as Live Oak are often deformed by direct exposure to salty air, but they survive and grow. Salt sensitive plants grow poorly or die when exposed to salty air.

Overhead wires

Trees are often planted too close to power lines. When branches reach overhead wires, the utility company must prune them to ensure uninterrupted utility service. It is best to plant trees as far away from utility wires as possible. Planting farther from the wires will allow you to choose from a greater variety of trees. When planting directly under, or within 6 feet of wires, select small-maturing trees or tall shrubs (see Appendix 3, p.157), or direct the tree to grow around the wire with regular pruning.

Soil pH

Parts of coastal Florida and many other areas throughout the state have alkaline soil. That is, the soil pH is above 7. Soil pH governs availability of nutrients to plants and also affects activity of soil microorganisms. If soil pH is above 7, micronutrient deficiencies develop in some plants. Plants such as Ixora, Sweetgum, Red Maple and the Queen Palm grow poorly in these soils. Some, like junipers and Wild Tamarind, prefer high soil pH. Choose plants that are adapted to high pH (alkaline) soils if the pH is above 7. Do not guess the pH. Have it tested! It is probably the most important component of the soil test. Be prepared to apply fertilizer containing micronutrients if your soil is alkaline.

Texture

Soil texture is more an indicator of other soil characteristics that influence plant growth than a growth limiting factor itself. For example, clay soils often drain poorly, especially if the terrain is flat and the soil was disturbed, such as around a new home. When planting in a clay or marl soil, pay particular attention to evaluating soil drainage. If drainage is poor, then choose plants that tolerate wet soil (see Appendix 4, p.157).

Sandy soils generally drain faster than clay soils. If irrigation will not be provided in a well-drained, sandy soil on a regular basis, after plants are established, drought tolerant plants should be chosen for the site. All plants, even those rated as drought tolerant, perform best with regular irrigation until well established. Plants in this book are rated for their tolerance to drought in a well-drained, sandy soil. Sandy soils also leach faster than clay soils, carrying nitrogen, potassium and other essential elements below the root zone. This will affect fertilization management in the established landscape. If you are not able to maintain a regular fertilization program, consider choosing species that are native to the sandy soil of the planting site. These plants are often better adapted to soils with low nutrient content.

Soil drainage

Poorly-drained, hard, or compacted soils contain little oxygen – a gas that plant roots need to survive and grow. Although clay, loam, or sandy soil can become compacted, compacted clay soil presents the biggest challenge for plants. Many die or grow poorly and succumb to an insect or disease problem because they are planted in soil that is too compacted, or too wet during certain times of the year. Only plants tolerant of wet sites can survive in these difficult soils (see Appendix 4, p.157).

Although a number of plants tolerate flooded soil conditions, they establish better and faster when the soil is moist, but well-drained. Flooding is tolerated once they become well-established. Only a few plants, such as Bald Cypress, Cordgrass and some others, can be established in flooded soil. Plants in their natural habitat are sometimes exposed to flooded soil in winter more often than summer. Some plants, indicated as tolerant of flooded or wet soil, could suffer if the entire root system is flooded for a long period of time in summer.

Soil depth

If bedrock comes close to the surface, leaving only a thin layer of soil on top, such as in parts of Dade and much of Monroe County, or if there is little soil, you may want to avoid planting large-maturing trees in the landscape. Large trees in shallow soil could topple over in storms as they grow older, especially if roots are restricted to an artificially small space. They also produce large roots that grow along the soil surface, causing disruption of mowing and gardening activities.

Personal preferences

After considering the cultural conditions at the planting site, you will narrow your list of possible plants to those that will grow well in that area. Now it is time to choose the desired look you would like your plants to have, such as showy flowers (Appendix 5, p.157, 158). Selecting plants only from those that will grow well at the site, is a sure way to improve plant performance and beauty in your yard.

Site preparation

The soil may need to be worked before plants can be set into the ground and planted. Proper site preparation may include grading, so water drains away from planting beds, loosening soil that is compacted, or adding soil amendments. Some soil amendments, added before planting, can temporarily change soil pH or improve structure and water-holding capacity. For example, composted yard waste, such as decomposed leaves and twigs, appears to be a good material for improving large planting beds containing groups of shrubs, perennials, ground covers and trees. Individual planting holes for trees or shrubs do not need amendments unless there is virtually no soil at the site. In this case, soil compensations are necessary to develop a medium for root growth.

TURFGRASS

Selection of the proper grass for your lawn depends on several factors, including the amount of sun, salt exposure, irrigation availability and expected foot traffic. All grass needs sun to form a dense turf. Although 'Delmar' and 'Seville' St. Augustine grass tolerates some shade, disease problems are fewer and growth is more vigorous in a sunny location. Centipede grass also tolerates some shade. Other turfgrasses are not suited for a partially shaded location. The best wearing grasses are Bahia grass and Bermuda grass. Others become thin with regular foot traffic. St. Augustine grass and Bermuda grass are best for landscapes along the coast, because of their tolerance for salt air. Bahia grass and Bermuda grass are the most drought tolerant grasses for lawns.

Cynodon dactylon (SIGH-no-don DAK-til-on)

Common name:
Bermuda Grass

Wear tolerance:
excellent

Mowing: 1/2-1 1/2"
every 3-5 days

Culture: poor shade
tolerance, acid to alkaline
pH, good salt and drought
tolerance

Notes: Bermuda grass is typically planted in athletic fields, not in home lawns. It is normally cut with a reel mower, which is not commonly purchased by homeowners (nearly all have rotary mowers). The edges of the turf (stolons and rhizomes) quickly grow into adjacent landscape beds and can become a weedy nuisance.

Eremochloa ophiuroides

(err-eh-moe-CHLOE-ah
oh-few-ROY-deez)

Common name:
Centipede Grass

Wear tolerance: poor

Mowing: 1 1/2-2" every
10-14 days

Culture: fair shade
tolerance, good drought
tolerance, salt sensitive

Notes: Centipede grass is only common in the panhandle of Florida. It is usually installed as sod, needs little mowing and maintains a neat appearance with minimum care. Regular fertilizer and irrigation can lead to the decline of centipede grass. Irrigation during fall and spring dry periods is beneficial. Nematode damage limits use in south Florida.

Lolium multiflorum (LO-li-um mul-ti-FLOR-um)

Common name:
Rye Grass
Wear tolerance: fair
Mowing: 2-3" when
needed
Culture: fair shade
tolerance, drought and salt
sensitive
Notes: Rye grass seed is
spread in the fall (when
high temperatures are less

than 80 degrees) to provide a light green color throughout winter and spring in the northern half of the state. After raking the lawn thoroughly, spread seeds evenly over existing St. Augustine grass or Bahia grass to hide the dormant brown color typical in winter. Water lightly and regularly until established. It can also be used to temporarily minimize erosion on bare soil in the cool season. It will not last through the summer in Florida. Rye grass begins to die as temperatures reach into the 80's in spring.

Paspalum notatum (Pass-PAY-lum noe-TAY-tum)

Common name:
Bahia Grass
Wear tolerance: poor
Mowing: 3-4" every
4-7 days
Culture: poor shade
tolerance, excellent drought
tolerance, acid to slightly
alkaline pH, salt sensitive
Notes: Bahia grass is only
suited for a landscape that

receives at least 6 hours of direct sun, although sun from dawn to dusk is preferred. It produces a thinner turf than St. Augustine grass. The most annoying characteristic is the seed heads that develop in warm weather, several days after mowing. 'Argentine' is usually more dense than other selections. Bahia grass is usually installed as sod, although it is occasionally seeded. Mole crickets pose the biggest pest problem.

Stenotaphrum secundatum

(sten-oh-TAH-frum see-
cun-DAY-tum)

Common name:
St. Augustine Grass
Wear tolerance: poor
Mowing: 2 1/2-4" every
4-7 days
Culture: fair shade
tolerance, good salt
tolerance, drought sensitive
Notes: St. Augustine grass

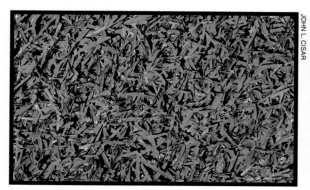

is best for a sunny location, although the cultivars 'Delmar' and 'Seville' are good selections for a partially shaded location. If you cannot provide at least 3 hours of sun, consider planting a shade tolerant ground cover instead. St. Augustine grass is usually installed as sod, although plugs can be placed 6-12" apart. Watch for chinch bugs in warm weather and worms or caterpillars in the fall. 'Floratam' and 'Floralawn' are resistant to chinch bugs.

Zoysia spp. (ZOY-see-ah species)

Common name:
Zoysia grass
Wear tolerance:
excellent
Mowing: 1-2" every
3-5 days
Culture: fair shade
tolerance, acid to alkaline
pH, good salt and drought
tolerance
Notes: Zoysia grass

establishes very slowly, but makes a fabulous lawn with proper care; susceptible to soil nematodes; is typically cut with a reel mower, which is not commonly purchased by homeowners (nearly all have rotary mowers). The edges of the turf (stolons and rhizomes) quickly grow into adjacent landscape beds and can become a weedy nuisance.

BEDDING PLANTS

With the exception of Impatiens and Flowering Tobacco, most bedding plants perform best in a sunny location. A planting project is often disappointing unless the location receives at least 4 hours of sun. Ample foliage can be produced in a shaded location but flowering is usually poor.

You might waste your time, money and effort if you plant in the wrong season. Just because a plant is offered for sale in a garden center, does not mean it should be planted at that time of year. For example, you might see Impatiens in a garden shop in north Florida in September, but plants could be killed if an early frost arrives in October.

Plants offered in 4" pots provide a quick effect in the landscape, but are more expensive than those in smaller plug trays. The smaller plants in trays are only about 2 weeks behind the 4" pots. Landscape soil should be prepared with a shovel and is often mixed with organic matter, such as peat moss, before planting. Some landscapers routinely mix in other soil amendments, such as water absorbing gels. Try not to walk on the soft bed of soil once it is ready for planting. To prevent soil compaction, some people kneel on a wide board to distribute their weight. Gently insert plants in a hole about as deep as the root ball, covering the sides with soil. Do not cover the top of the root ball with soil, as plants could dry out.

Water regularly for several weeks after planting, but do not saturate the soil, as roots could rot. Apply frequent, light applications, keeping the soil moist throughout the growing season. Irrigation can be applied less often to winter annuals (those planted in fall through winter) than summer annuals (those planted in spring through summer). Once plants are established, irrigation in winter may not be required in north Florida.

B E D D I N G   P L A N T S

Antirrhinum majus (an-ter-RYE-num MAY-juss)

Common name:
Snapdragon
Cold tolerance: hardy
Size: 6-24" tall; fast
growth; 6 to 12" spacing
Form: upright/erect;
green foliage
Flower: showy; red,
yellow, white, pink, orange,
salmon, lavender or purple
Culture: full sun to
partial shade; water regularly; low salt
tolerance; pest resistant; plant fall and winter
in south Florida; fall or spring in the north
Notes: tolerates temperatures to about 20
degrees but with reduced flowering; stops
flowering in hot weather; cultivars are
available with heights from 6-24" tall
Uses: border, mass planting, container, cut
flowers and edging

Begonia x semperflorens-cultorum

(bee-GO-nee-uh x
sem-per-FLOR-renz-cull-
TOR-rum)
Common name: Wax
Begonia, Fibrous Begonia
Cold tolerance: tender
Size: 6-18" tall; slow
growth; 6 to 12" spacing
Form: round; green,
purple/red, (occasionally
variegated) foliage
Flower: showy; red, white, pink or salmon
Culture: full sun to partial shade; pest
resistant; water regularly; low salt tolerance;
plant fall through early spring in south
Florida; after frost in the north
Notes: planted as much for the foliage color
as for the flower effect; very hot weather in
south Florida reduces vigor
Uses: edging, mass planting, container,
hanging basket

Catharanthus roseus (kath-uh-RANTH-us ROE-zee-us)

Common name: Periwinkle, Vinca, Madagascar Periwinkle

Cold tolerance: tender

Size: 1-2' tall; fast growth; 12 to 18" spacing

Form: spreading and rounded; green foliage

Flower: showy; white, pink, purple or lavender

Culture: full sun to partial shade; high salt tolerance; high drought tolerance once established; planted year round in south Florida, after frost in the north

Notes: escapes cultivation and can become a weed; susceptible to root rot if over-irrigated; plant in well-drained soil

Uses: container, edging, groundcover, mass planting, hanging basket

Celosia plumosa (see-LOE-see-uh ploo-MOE-suh)

Common name: Cockscomb

Cold tolerance: tender

Size: 6-24" tall; moderate growth; 6 to 12" spacing

Form: upright/erect; green, purple/red foliage

Flower: showy; red, yellow, pink, purple or orange

Culture: full sun; water regularly; pest resistant; planted year round in south Florida, after frost in the north

Notes: does best in a sunny, sheltered location in fertile, well-drained soil; often self-seeds in the landscape

Uses: border, edging, mass planting, container

Dianthus spp. (dye-ANTH-us species)

Common name:
Dianthus
Cold tolerance: hardy
Size: 6-12" tall; slow
growth; 6 to 12" spacing
Form: round; green
foliage
Flower: showy; red,
white or pink
Culture: full sun to
partial shade; water

regularly; medium salt tolerance; pest
sensitive; plant in fall and winter in south
Florida, in fall or spring in the north
Notes: continues to flower with
temperatures in the 20's; stops flowering in very hot weather; caterpillars occasionally eat
foliage
Uses: container, attracts butterflies, border,
edging

Evolvulus glomeratus (ee-VOLV-yoo-luss glom-mer-RAY-tuss)

Common name:
Blue Daze
Cold tolerance: tender
Size: 6-12" tall; moderate
growth; 12 to 18" spacing
Form: spreading, round;
green, blue-green foliage
Flower: showy; blue
Culture: full sun to
partial shade; high salt
tolerance; medium drought

tolerance; pest resistant; plant year round in
south Florida, after frost in the north
Notes: where there is no frost, plants last
for more than one year; cut back in spring if
needed; flowers open in the morning, and close in the afternoon; die-out in center of
plant caused by fungus in summer
Uses: groundcover, mass planting, border,
edging, container, hanging basket, cascade
effect

B E D D I N G   P L A N T S

Gaillardia pulchella (gay-LAR-dee-uh pul-KELL-luh)

Common name: Gaillardia, Blanket-Flower
Cold tolerance: hardy
Size: 1-2' tall; moderate growth; 12 to 18" spacing
Form: round, spreading; green foliage
Flower: showy; red, yellow and orange
Culture: full sun; high salt tolerance; high drought tolerance; pest resistant; plant year round in south Florida, after frost in the north
Notes: hardy throughout the state, but stops flowering in winter; several selections have been made for flower color and plant height
Uses: dune stabilization, container, cut flowers, accent, mass planting, groundcover, attracts butterflies

Helianthus annuus (heel-lee-ANTH-us AN-yoo-us)

Common name: Common Sunflower
Cold tolerance: hardy
Size: 2-10' tall; 1-2' wide; fast growth; 18-24" spacing
Form: upright/erect; green foliage; gray, edible fruit
Flower: very showy; yellow, orange; 3 months after planting seed
Culture: full sun; acid to slightly alkaline pH; water regularly; medium salt tolerance; low drought tolerance; pest sensitive
Notes: plant dies following the spectacular flower display; may need staking; dwarf cultivars are available in a variety of sizes
Uses: specimen, accent, mass planting, attracts butterflies

Impatiens x **New Guinea Hybrids** (im-PAY-shenz)

Common name:
New Guinea Impatiens
Cold tolerance: tender
Size: 1-2' tall; fast growth;
12 to 18" spacing
Form: round, spreading;
variegated, purple/red/
yellow foliage
Flower: showy; pink,
white, red, lavender, orange
or purple

Culture: mostly shade; requires regular watering; pest resistant; plant fall and winter in south Florida, after frost in the north
Notes: cool season annual in south Florida, a warm season annual for the north, best in shade; melts out in summer in south Florida; many varieties will take full winter sun in south Florida
Uses: border, edging, mass planting, container, attracts butterflies, interiors

Impatiens wallerana (im-PAY-shenz wall-ler-RAY-nuh)

Common name:
Impatiens
Cold tolerance: tender
Size: 1-2' tall; fast growth;
12 to 18" spacing
Form: round, spreading;
green or variegated foliage
Flower: showy; red,
white, pink, salmon, purple,
lavender or orange

Culture: partial shade to full shade; requires regular watering in hot weather; pest resistant; plant fall and winter in south Florida, after frost in the north
Notes: cool season annual for sun or shade in south Florida, warm season annual for the shade in the north; melts out in south Florida in summer
Uses: edging, mass planting, container, hanging basket, border, attracts butterflies, interiors

Lobularia maritima (lob-ew-LAH-ree-a ma-RI-ti-ma)

Common name:
Sweet Alyssum
Cold tolerance: half-hardy (tolerates light frost)
Size: 6″ tall; slow growth; 6-12″ spacing
Form: spreading; delicate green foliage
Flower: small, abundant and showy; white, pink, lavender; intensely fragrant

Culture: full sun to part shade; water regularly; fertile, well-drained soil; stops flowering in hot weather
Notes: cascades over a wall or down the side of a container
Uses: edging, container or annual ground-cover for the cooler months

Nicotiana alata (nick-koe-shee-AY-nuh uh-LAY-tuh)

Common name:
Nicotiana, Flowering Tobacco, Ornamental Tobacco
Cold tolerance: tender
Size: 1-3′ tall; moderate growth; 12 to 18″ spacing
Form: upright/erect; green foliage
Flower: showy; red, white, pink or salmon

Culture: partial shade; fertile, well-drained soil; pest resistant; plant in fall or winter in south Florida, spring or fall in the north for a short burst of color
Notes: summer sun melts plants
Uses: mass planting, border, cut flowers, attracts hummingbirds

B E D D I N G   P L A N T S

Pelargonium x hortorum (pell-lar-GO-nee-um hor-TOR-rum)

Common name: Geranium

Cold tolerance: tender

Size: 1-2' tall; moderate growth; 18 to 24" spacing

Form: round, upright/erect; green foliage

Flower: showy; red, pink, white, salmon or orange

Culture: full sun (in winter) to partial shade; medium salt and drought tolerance; pest resistant; plant fall and winter in south Florida, fall or spring in the north

Notes: flowers best in spring and fall in the north, and from fall through the winter and spring in south Florida; don't overwater

Uses: container, mass planting, hanging basket, border

Petunia x hybrida (puh-TOON-nee-uh HI-brid-duh)

Common name: Petunia

Cold tolerance: hardy

Size: 12-18" tall; moderate growth; 6 to 12" spacing

Form: spreading; green foliage

Flower: showy; red, yellow, white, pink, salmon, purple or lavender

Culture: full sun; fertile, well-drained soil; pest resistant; plant in fall and winter in south Florida, fall or spring in the north

Notes: survives temperatures to about 20 degrees, but flowering stops for several weeks after a frost; flowering stops in hot weather; roots rot if soil is kept too wet

Uses: mass planting, container, edging, hanging basket, cascade effect

Salvia farinacea (SAL-vee-uh fair-rin-NAY-see-uh)

Common name:
Blue Salvia, Mealycup Sage,
Blue Sage
Cold tolerance: tender
Size: 2-3' tall; fast growth;
6 to 12" spacing
Form: upright/erect;
green foliage
Flower: showy; blue
or white
Culture: full sun to part

shade; high salt tolerance; water regularly; fertile, well-drained soil; pest resistant; plant year-round in south Florida, after frost in the north
Notes: cut plants back if they become leggy; cultivars available with blue or white flowers; plants can act like a perennial
Uses: mass planting, border, cut flowers, attracts butterflies and hummingbirds

Salvia splendens (SAL-vee-uh SPLEN-denz)

Common name:
Red Salvia, Scarlet Salvia,
Scarlet Sage
Cold tolerance: tender
Size: 1-3' tall; moderate
growth; 6 to 12" spacing
Form: upright/erect,
round; green foliage
Flower: showy; red,
white, salmon, purple, pink
or lavender

Culture: full sun to partial shade; water regularly; medium salt tolerance; fertile, well-drained soil; pest resistant; plant year round in south Florida, after frost in the north
Notes: cut back after flowering for a uniform second flower display
Uses: edging, container, mass planting

Tagetes erecta (tuh-JEE-teez ee-RECK-tuh)

Common name:
Marigold
Cold tolerance: tender
Size: 1-3' tall; moderate
growth; 12 to 18" spacing
Form: upright/erect;
green foliage
Flower: showy; yellow,
orange
Culture: full sun; water
regularly; medium salt
tolerance; fertile, well-drained soil; pest
sensitive; plant year round in south Florida,
after frost in the north
Notes: mites often infest and destroy plants,
especially in hot, dry weather
Uses: mass planting, container or planter,
edging, cut flowers, border, attracts butterflies

Tithonia rotundifolia (tith-OH-nee-uh roe-tun-diff-FOLE-lee-uh)

Common name:
Mexican Sunflower
Cold tolerance: tender
Size: 3-6' tall; rapid
growth; 24 to 36" spacing
Form: upright/erect;
green foliage
Flower: showy; orange
Culture: full sun; high
drought tolerance; fertile,
well-drained soil; pest
resistant; plant year round in south Florida,
after frost in the north
Notes: flowers profusely for two or three
months before dying; plants grow rapidly
once they become established
Uses: attracts butterflies, mass planting,
border, accent

Verbena x hybrida (ver-BEEN-nuh HI-brid-duh)

Common name: Garden Verbena, Hybrid Verbena

Cold tolerance: tender

Size: 6-12" tall; moderate growth; 24 to 36" spacing

Form: spreading, upright/erect, round; green foliage

Flower: showy; pink, purple, white or lavender

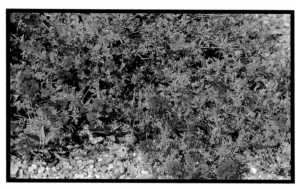

Culture: full sun; well-drained to moderately dry soil; medium drought tolerance; pest resistant; plant year round in south Florida, after frost in the north

Notes: many verbena species are available, including a native species

Uses: container, mass planting, attracts butterflies, cascade effect, hanging basket, edging, cut flowers

Viola x wittrockiana (vye-OH-luh wit-rock-kee-AY-nuh)

Common name: Pansy

Cold tolerance: hardy

Size: 6-12" tall; slow growth; 6 to 12" spacing

Form: round, spreading; green foliage

Flower: showy; red, yellow, white, blue, pink, purple, orange or lavender

Culture: full sun to

partial shade; water regularly in warm weather; pest resistant; plant in fall and winter; plants melt in hot weather

Notes: continues to flower in temperatures as low as 20 degrees

Uses: mass planting, container or planter, edging, cut flowers, border

PERENNIALS

Many perennials are probably adapted to Florida landscapes, but relatively few have been tried. Each year, we see more and more available at local garden centers around the state. Some of the 'tried-and-true' ones are presented here. With a little planning, you can have flowers in your garden year-round, even in most regions of north Florida. They are typically offered in the spring at garden centers and are usually best planted at this time.

Summer flowering types come into bloom soon after planting in spring, followed by the fall flowering Firespike, Philippine Violet and others. Some grow year round in south Florida but are killed to the ground (roots survive) in the north. Start with the types discussed below, then move on to others available at your local stores. Ordering by catalogue from another state is risky because plants may perform poorly here. You can be fairly certain that plants at local nurseries have received some testing for their durability under Florida conditions, especially if the retail garden center purchased from a Florida grower.

Alpinia zerumbet 'Variegata'

(al-PIN-nee-uh
zair-rum-BET)

Common name:
Variegated Shellflower,
Variegated Shell Ginger
Zone: 10a-11
Size: 4-7' tall; 5-8' wide;
moderate growth; 24 to 36"
spacing
Form: upright/erect;
yellow and green
variegated foliage

Flower: showy; white; summer
Culture: full sun to partial shade; tolerates occasional wet soil; acid to slightly alkaline pH; medium salt tolerance; pest resistant
Notes: these plants like moisture; bright yellow and green foliage catches the eye; plants killed in winter in north Florida usually emerge in spring and look fine by the summer
Uses: planter, specimen, border, mass planting, accent, indoors

Asclepias tuberosa (as-KLEEP-pee-ass too-ber-ROE-suh)

Common name:
Butterfly Weed, Indian
Paintbrush
Zone: 4-10a; Florida
native
Size: 2-3' tall and wide;
moderate growth; 18 to 24"
spacing
Form: upright/erect at
first then rounded; green
foliage

Flower: showy; orange, red and yellow; summer
Culture: full sun; acid pH; medium salt tolerance; medium drought tolerance; pest sensitive
Notes: seedlings germinate readily in the landscape causing a potential weed problem; aphids can reduce the flower display dramatically
Uses: border, naturalizing, cut flowers, attracts butterflies, mass planting

Barleria cristata (bar-LEER-ree-uh kriss-STAY-tuh)

Common name:
Philippine Violet, Bluebell
Barleria, Barleria
Zone: 10b-11
Size: 4-8' tall and wide;
fast growth; 36 to 60"
spacing
Form: upright/erect then
rounded; green foliage
Flower: very showy;
lavender, pink, and

sometimes white; summer and fall
Culture: full sun to partial shade; acid to
slightly alkaline pH; medium salt tolerance;
medium drought tolerance; pest resistant
Notes: plants fill with flowers in late
summer until frost arrives, or in spring in
south Florida; lightly prune after flowers fade
to encourage more flowers; plants become
woody and can last many years in south
Florida; self-seeding in south Florida
Uses: container or planter, hedge,
foundation, border

Caladium x hortulanum (kuh-LAY-dee-um x hor-too-LAY-num)

Common name:
Caladium
Zone: 9-11
Size: 1-2' tall and wide;
fast growth; 6 to 12"
spacing
Form: upright/erect;
variegated, purple, red, pink
and green foliage
Flower: hidden by
foliage; white; summer

Culture: partial to full shade; acid pH; low
salt tolerance; low drought tolerance; pest
sensitive; foliage burns in full sun
Notes: fabulous color item for total shade
Uses: mass planting, container or planter,
ground cover, edging, border, indoors in a
shallow pot

Canna x generalis (KAN-nuh jen-ner-AL-liss)

Common name:
Canna, Garden Canna

Zone: 8a-11

Size: 2-5′ tall; 1-2′ wide; fast growth; 12 to 18″ spacing

Form: upright/erect; green, purple/red, occasionally variegated foliage

Flower: showy; red, orange, yellow or pink; summer

Culture: full sun; acid to slightly alkaline pH; medium salt tolerance; medium drought tolerance; pest sensitive

Notes: *C. flaccida* is native to Florida; cut back foliage as it dies but leave plants in the ground to come back the following year

Uses: mass planting, container or planter, border

Coreopsis spp. (kor-ree-OP-sis species)

Common name:
Tickseed, Coreopsis

Zone: 4a-10b; Florida native

Size: 1-3′ tall and wide; moderate growth; 6 to 12″ spacing

Form: upright/erect; green foliage

Flower: showy; yellow (most common), red, pink, purple or orange; summer

Culture: full sun; acid to slightly alkaline pH; medium salt tolerance; high drought tolerance; pest and disease sensitive

Notes: *C. leavenworthii* (yellow) is native; many others are available at garden centers

Uses: border, edging, mass planting, attracts butterflies

Cortaderia selloana (kor-tuh-DEER-ree-uh sell-loe-AY-nuh)

Common name:
Pampas Grass
Zone: 8-11
Size: 8-10' tall and wide;
fast growth; 6-10' spacing
Form: round,
upright/erect; green foliage;
showy, tan fruit
Flower: showy; creamy
white or pink; summer and
fall

Culture: full sun to partial shade; acid to alkaline pH; moderate salt tolerance; high drought tolerance; pest resistant

Notes: plant is too big for most residential landscapes; substitute with the native Fakahatchee Grass; cut back in late winter to remove brown leaves; razor sharp leaf margins; plants occasionally escape cultivation and can become a fire hazard

Uses: screen, border, mass planting, specimen, accent, cut flowers, best for large commercial landscapes

Crinum spp. (KRYE-num species)

Common name:
Crinum Lily
Zone: 8b-11
Size: 3-6' tall and wide;
moderate growth; 36 to 60"
spacing
Form: upright/erect;
green or purple foliage;
showy, green fruit
Flower: showy and
fragrant; white, purple,
pink, red

Culture: full sun to partial shade; some tolerate wet soil; acid to slightly alkaline pH; medium salt tolerance; medium drought tolerance; some are disease sensitive

Notes: plants are poisonous; *C. x amabile* has dark greenish to purple foliage and purple flowers; *C. americanum* is native to wet sites in Florida and has white flowers; *C. asiaticum* has white and pink flowers and is poisonous

Uses: border, mass planting, specimen, accent

Cuphea hyssopifolia (KOO-fee-uh hiss-sop-piff-FOLE-lee-uh)

Common name: False Heather, Mexican Heather, Heather

Zone: 10b-11

Size: 1-2' tall; 2-3' wide; moderate growth; 24 to 36" spacing

Form: vase, spreading; green foliage

Flower: showy; purple, lavender, pink or white; year-round in south Florida

Culture: full sun to partial shade; acid to alkaline pH; medium salt tolerance; high drought tolerance; pest sensitive

Notes: killed to the ground by hard freeze; cut back in north Florida in late winter before new growth emerges; if needed, cut back in south Florida to stimulate vigorous growth and renew flowering; seed dropped from existing plants germinate readily in the landscape

Uses: ground cover, naturalizing, edging, miniature hedge, border, mass planting, attracts butterflies

Dietes vegeta (dye-EE-teez VEDGE-jet-tuh)

Common name: African Iris, Butterfly Iris

Zone: 9-11

Size: 2-6' tall; 2' wide; slow growth; 24 to 36" spacing

Form: upright/erect; green foliage; green fruit

Flower: showy; white; periodically during the year

Culture: full sun to partial shade; tolerates wet, well-drained soil; acid to slightly alkaline pH; low salt tolerance; medium drought tolerance; pest resistant

Notes: frequent watering encourages flowering; after a cold winter in north Florida, cut brown foliage to several inches above ground before growth emerges in spring

Uses: specimen, border, mass planting, container or planter, naturalizing, accent, indoors

Gazania spp. (gay-ZAY-nee-uh species)

Common name:
Gazania
Zone: 8-10b
Size: 6-12" tall; 1-2' wide;
moderate growth; 12"
spacing
Form: round, spreading;
green foliage
Flower: showy; red,
yellow, white, pink, orange
or rust/bronze; summer

Culture: full sun only; acid to alkaline pH; medium salt tolerance; high drought tolerance; pest resistant
Notes: many cultivars are available; roots rot from over-watering and heavy rain; provide good drainage on a raised bed in a sunny location
Uses: mass planting, ground cover, edging, container

Hedychium coronarium

(hee-DICK-kee-um
kor-roe-NAIR-ree-um)
Common name:
Butterfly Ginger
Zone: 9-11
Size: 4-6' tall and wide;
fast growth; 24 to 36"
spacing
Form: upright/erect at
first then floppy; green
foliage

Flower: showy and extremely fragrant; white; summer
Culture: full sun to partial shade; tolerates flooding; acid to slightly alkaline pH; medium salt tolerance; low drought tolerance; pest resistant
Notes: these plants like moisture; a number of other gingers are available at local garden centers and through catalogues
Uses: accent, border, mass planting, indoors in bright light

P E R E N N I A L S

Heliconia caribaea (hell-lick-KOE-nee-uh kuh-RIB-bee-uh)

Common name: Caribbean Heliconia,
Wild Plantain
Zone: 10b-11
Size: 10-15' tall; 3-6' wide; fast growth;
36 to 60" spacing
Form: upright/erect; green foliage; blue fruit
Flower: very showy; green, red and yellow
Culture: full sun to partial shade; acid to
alkaline pH; medium salt tolerance; medium
drought tolerance; pest resistant
Notes: numerous books are available on the
many cultivated Heliconias; a tall clumping
perennial with showy flowers on second
year stalks
Uses: specimen, cut flowers, indoors

Hemerocallis spp. (hem-mer-roe-KAL-liss species)

Common name:
Daylily
Zone: 5-10b
Size: 1-3' tall; 1-2' wide;
moderate growth; 12 to 18"
spacing
Form: upright/erect;
green foliage
Flower: showy; orange,
purple, red, yellow,
lavender, pink, salmon;
spring and summer

Culture: full sun to partial shade; acid to
slightly alkaline pH; medium to high salt
tolerance; high drought tolerance; pest
resistant
Notes: hundreds of cultivars with an
endless variety of flower colors are available
from catalogues and garden centers; not all
do well in south Florida
Uses: edging, ground cover, border,
naturalizing, mass planting, attracts butterflies

31

Hippeastrum x *hybridum* (hip-pee-ASS-trum HI-brid-dum)

Common name:
Amaryllis
Zone: 8-10b
Size: 1-2' tall; slow growth; 6 to 12" spacing
Form: upright/erect; green foliage; green fruit
Flower: showy; red, orange, pink or white; spring
Culture: partial shade;

acid pH; low salt tolerance; medium drought tolerance; pest sensitive
Notes: plants flower poorly in too much shade; may require winter rest to flower well; bulbs can be left in the ground over winter in Florida; plants selected by Florida nurseries are more perennial than those from overseas
Uses: ground cover, mass planting, container or planter, border, naturalizing

Justicia brandegeana (juss-TISH-shee-uh bran-dedge-jee-AY-nuh)

Common name:
Shrimp Plant
Zone: 8b-11
Size: 2-4' tall and wide; moderate growth; 24 to 36" spacing
Form: spreading, upright/erect; green foliage
Flower: showy; red, yellow; nearly year-round
Culture: full sun to

shade; acid to slightly alkaline pH; low salt tolerance; medium drought tolerance; pest resistant
Notes: although 20 degrees kills plants to the ground, they re-emerge and flower in spring; stems root when they touch the ground and can be transplanted easily
Uses: border, mass planting, specimen, container or planter, naturalizing, attracts hummingbirds and butterflies

Justicia carnea (juss-TISH-shee-uh KAR-nee-uh)

Common name:
Jacobinia, Flamingo Plant
Zone: 9b-11
Size: 3-5' tall; 2-3' wide;
slow growth; 24 to 36"
spacing
Form: upright/erect,
spreading; green foliage
Flower: showy; pink, less
frequently white
Culture: partial to full

shade; acid to slightly alkaline pH; low salt tolerance; low drought tolerance; pest sensitive
Notes: a perennial that flowers periodically all year in south Florida and in the warm months in the north; caterpillars occasionally eat foliage; watch for mealybugs; killed to the ground at 20 degrees but emerges in spring; use as an annual in north Florida
Uses: foundation, border, mass planting, container or planter, cut flowers

Nymphaea spp. (nim-FEE-uh species)

Common name:
Waterlily
Zone: 3a-11;
Florida native
Size: 6-12" tall; 2-8' wide;
fast growth; 36 to 60"
spacing
Form: green foliage
Flower: showy; yellow,
white, pink or red; summer
Culture: full sun for best

flowering; low salt tolerance; low drought tolerance; pest resistant
Notes: *N. mexicana* (yellow flowers) and *N. odorata* (white flowers) are native to Florida; many hybrids are available in a variety of flower colors and plant sizes; select hardy waterlilies for north Florida; tropical varieties for south Florida
Uses: water garden, cut flowers, attracts butterflies

Pennisetum setaceum (pen-niss-SEE-tum set-TAY-see-um)

Common name:
Fountain Grass
Zone: 8a-10b
Size: 4-6' tall; 2-4' wide;
fast growth; 36 to 60"
spacing
Form: round,
upright/erect; green foliage
Flower: showy; white;
summer

Culture: full sun; acid to
slightly alkaline pH; low salt tolerance;
medium drought tolerance; pest resistant
Notes: the variety 'Rubrum' with red foliage
and flowers is more commonly planted in
some regions of Florida; 25 degrees kills
plants to the ground; can escape cultivation
and become a fire hazard
Uses: specimen, mass planting, container or
planter, accent, border, cut flowers

Pentas lanceolata (PEN-tuss lan-see-oh-LAY-tuh)

Common name:
Pentas
Zone: 9-11
Size: 2-3' tall and wide;
fast growth; 18 to 24"
spacing
Form: round; green
foliage
Flower: showy; red,
pink, lavender, white or
purple; nearly year-round

Culture: full sun to partial shade; acid pH;
low salt tolerance; low drought tolerance; pest
resistant
Notes: freezing temperatures kill plant to
the ground; flowering continues year-round
in south Florida where plants are
occasionally trimmed into hedges; plant any
time in south Florida
Uses: border, container, hanging basket,
small hedge, cut flowers, accent, attracts
butterflies

Pontederia cordata (pon-te DE-ree-a kor-DAH-ta)

Common name: Pickerel Weed
Zone: 3-10b
Size: 2-4'tall; medium growth rate; 24" spacing
Form: clumping; green foliage
Flower: showy; blue-purple; summer to fall
Culture: full sun; acid to alkaline pH; low salt tolerance; low drought tolerance; pest resistant
Notes: use in contained pools or around shallow edges of ponds; spreads rapidly; white forms available
Uses: water garden; waterbody edges; wetland restoration

Stachytarpheta jamaicensis

(stake-kee-tar-FEE-tuh jah-may-SEN-sis)
Common name:
Blue Porterweed
Zone: 10a-11
Size: 4-8' tall and wide; fast growth; 36 to 60" spacing
Form: round; green foliage
Flower: showy; blue; in warm months
Culture: full sun to partial shade; acid to alkaline pH; high drought tolerance; pest resistant
Notes: plants are relatively open and grow larger than many other perennials; stems grow to an inch or more in diameter and become woody; pink flowering Porterweed is also available; flowers close at night
Uses: hedge or screen, border, mass planting, attracts butterflies

⬤P E R E N N I A L S

Strelitzia reginae (strell-LITZ-zee-uh ree-JIN-nee)

Common name:
Bird of Paradise
Zone: 10a-11
Size: 3-5' tall; 2-4' wide;
slow growth; 24 to 36"
spacing
Form: upright/erect;
green to blue-green foliage
Flower: very showy;
orange and blue;
periodically throughout the
year

Culture: full sun to partial shade; tolerates occasional wet soil; acid to slightly alkaline pH; low salt tolerance; high drought tolerance; pest sensitive

Notes: plants attract a great deal of attention due to the striking flowers and stiff, upright habit
Uses: border, mass planting, specimen, container or planter, accent

Tripsacum dactyloides (trip-SAY-kum dack-till-LOY-deez)

Common name:
Fakahatchee Grass,
Gamma Grass,
Eastern Gamma Grass
Zone: 5a-11: Florida
native
Size: 4-6' tall and wide;
moderate growth; 36 to 60"
spacing
Form: round; green
foliage

Flower: not showy; red and yellow
Culture: full sun to partial shade; tolerates wet soil; acid to slightly alkaline pH; medium salt tolerance; medium drought tolerance; pest resistant

Notes: *T. floridana* is smaller with thinner leaves and a fine texture
Uses: accent, border, mass planting, great substitute for Pampas Grass

G R O U N D C O V E R S

Dryopteris erythrosora (dry-OP-teer-riss air-rith-roe-SOR-ruh)

Common name:
Autumn Fern, Japanese
Shield Fern, Japanese Wood
Fern

Zone: 8-11

Size: 1-2' tall and wide;
slow growth; 18 to 24"
spacing

Form: upright/erect;
evergreen, green foliage;
brown spores

Flower: no flowers; plants reproduce by
spores

Culture: partial to full shade; acid pH; low
salt tolerance; low drought tolerance; pest
resistant

Notes: new foliage emerges reddish-bronze
then turns green; provides a rich texture to
the shaded landscape

Uses: groundcover, mass planting, edging

Gardenia jasminoides 'Prostrata'

(gar-DEEN-nee-uh
jass-min-NOY-deez)

Common name:
Dwarf Gardenia

Zone: 8a-10b

Size: 2-3' tall; 3-6' wide;
moderate growth; 24 to 36"
spacing

Form: spreading,
prostrate (flat); evergreen,
green foliage

Flower: showy and fragrant; white;
summer

Culture: full sun to partial shade; acid pH;
low salt tolerance; low drought tolerance; pest
sensitive

Notes: forms a thick groundcover, especially
in the sun; variegated cultivar exists

Uses: bonsai, groundcover, container, mass
planting, cascade effect

G R O U N D C O V E R S

Gelsemium sempervirens

(jell-SEEM-mee-um
sem-per-VYE-renz)

Common name:
Carolina Yellow Jasmine

Zone: 7a-9b; Florida
native

Size: 1' tall; variable
spread; fast growth; 24 to
36" spacing

Form: spreading;
deciduous, green foliage;
brown fruit

Flower: showy and fragrant; yellow; late
winter

Culture: full sun to partial shade; tolerates
occasional wet soil; acid to slightly alkaline
pH; low salt tolerance; medium drought

tolerance; pest resistant

Notes: plants climb up into shrubs and
trees growing to 40' tall; very poisonous

Uses: groundcover, mass planting,
naturalizing, container, hanging basket, vine

Hedera canariensis (HED-der-ruh kuh-nair-ree-EN-sis)

Common name:
Algerian Ivy

Zone: 8b-10b

Size: 6" tall; variable
spread; fast growth; 18 to
24" spacing

Form: spreading,
prostrate (flat) vine; green
foliage

Flower: not showy;
creamy white

Culture: partial to full shade; acid pH;
medium salt tolerance; medium drought
tolerance; pest resistant

Notes: makes a rich groundcover in the

shade; variegated cultivar is popular in some
regions; climbs onto walls and into trees

Uses: groundcover, mass planting, container,
hanging basket, indoors, cut foliage

G R O U N D C O V E R S

Hedera helix (HED-der-ruh HELL-licks)

Common name:
English Ivy
Zone: 5a-9b
Size: 6" tall; variable
spread; fast growth once
established; 18 to 24"
spacing
Form: spreading,
prostrate (flat) vine;
evergreen, green foliage
Flower: not showy;
creamy white
Culture: partial to full shade; acid pH;
medium salt tolerance; medium drought
tolerance; pest resistant
Notes: hundreds of cultivars are available

for foliage color, shape and size; plants are
easily damaged by walking on them;
poisonous
Uses: groundcover, mass planting, container,
hanging basket, indoors, cut foliage

Helianthus debilis (heel-lee-ANTH-us DEB-bill-liss)

Common name:
Beach Sunflower
Zone: 8b-11; Florida
native
Size: 1-2' tall; fast growth;
18 to 24" spacing
Form: prostrate (flat),
spreading; semi-evergreen,
green foliage
Flower: showy; yellow
Culture: full sun; acid to

alkaline pH; high salt tolerance; high drought
tolerance; pest resistant
Notes: temperatures in the 20's kill plants to
the ground

Uses: dune stabilization, groundcover,
attracts butterflies, border, mass planting,
cascade effect

43

Juniperus chinensis 'Parsonii'

(joo-NIP-per-russ chin-
EN-sis)

Common name:
Parson's Juniper
Zone: 7a-10b
Size: 2-3' tall; 4-10' wide;
moderate growth; 36 to 60"
spacing
Form: prostrate (flat),
spreading; evergreen,
blue-green to green foliage

Flower: not showy
Culture: full sun to partial shade; acid to
alkaline pH; high salt tolerance; high drought
tolerance; pest resistant

Notes: full sun required for fullest plants;
variegated cultivar is available
Uses: foundation, mass planting,
groundcover, bonsai

Juniperus conferta (joo-NIP-per-russ kawn-FER-tuh)

Common name:
Shore Juniper
Zone: 6a-10b
Size: 12-18" tall; 6-10'
wide; slow growth; 36 to
60" spacing
Form: spreading,
prostrate (flat); evergreen,
blue/blue-green foliage;
blue fruit
Flower: not showy

Culture: full sun; acid to alkaline pH;
excellent salt tolerance; high drought
tolerance; sensitive to fungus blight, especially
away from the beach
Notes: soft textured groundcover especially

suited for the coastal communities;
'Compacta' is slightly shorter and more dense;
place in full sun for best growth
Uses: dune stabilization, groundcover, mass
planting, cascade effect

Juniperus horizontalis (joo-NIP-per-russ hor-riz-zon-TAY-liss)

Common name:
Horizontal Juniper
Zone: 3a-9a
Size: less than 1' tall;
8-10' wide; moderate
growth; 36 to 60" spacing
Form: spreading,
prostrate (flat); evergreen,
green to blue-green foliage;
blue fruit
Flower: not showy

Culture: full sun; acid to alkaline pH; low to medium salt tolerance; high drought tolerance; pest resistant
Notes: 'Bar Harbor' and 'Blue Rug' are popular in some regions of central and north Florida; plants become thin in partial shade
Uses: mass planting, groundcover, hanging basket, cascade effect, bonsai

Juniperus chinensis procumbens **'Nana'**

(joo-NIP-per-russ chin-
EN-sis pro-KUM-benz)
Common name:
Dwarf Procumbens Juniper,
Dwarf Japgarden Juniper
Zone: 5a-10b
Size: 6-12" tall; 5-8' wide;
slow growth; 36 to 60"
spacing
Form: prostrate (flat),
spreading; evergreen, green
foliage
Flower: not showy
Culture: full sun to partial shade; acid to alkaline pH; medium salt tolerance; high drought tolerance; pest resistant

Notes: full sun is best to minimize disease problems; plants form an irregular mound of fine-textured foliage
Uses: mass planting, cut foliage, cascade effect, groundcover, bonsai

Lantana montevidensis (lan-TAY-nuh mon-tiv-vid-DEN-sis)

Common name:
Trailing Lantana, Purple Lantana, Weeping Lantana
Zone: 10b-11
Size: 2-3' tall; 4-8' wide; fast growth; 36 to 60" spacing
Form: spreading, prostrate (flat); evergreen (south Florida) green foliage; green fruit

Flower: showy; lavender, pink, white; spring through fall
Culture: full sun to partial shade; acid to alkaline pH; high salt tolerance; medium to high drought tolerance; pest sensitive
Notes: frost kills plants to the ground but they come back in spring; plants eventually become woody and look best when cut back nearly to the ground in late winter; leaf spots cause defoliation in partial shade
Uses: groundcover, mass planting, container, cut flowers, hanging basket, attracts butterflies, cascade effect

Lantana camara **'Gold Mound'** (lan-TAY-nuh kuh-MAIR-uh)

Common name:
Gold Mound' Lantana
Zone: 9a-11
Size: 2-3' tall; 4-6' wide; fast growth; 36-60" spacing
Form: round, spreading; evergreen (south Florida) green foliage; black, purple, green fruit
Flower: showy; yellow-orange; spring through fall; nearly year-round in south Florida

Culture: full sun; acid to alkaline pH; medium salt tolerance; high drought tolerance; pest sensitive
Notes: a native lantana with similar characteristics may be available at some local garden centers; caterpillars can devour foliage and reduce flowering; comes back from roots in spring in north Florida
Uses: border, mass planting, container, groundcover, foundation, cut flowers, attracts butterflies, cascade effect, hanging basket

G R O U N D C O V E R S

Liriope muscari (luh-RYE-oh-pee mus-KAR-ree)

Common name:
Lilyturf, Liriope, Border
Grass

Zone: 6a-10b

Size: 6-12" tall; 1-2' wide;
moderate growth; 6 to 12"
spacing

Form: upright/erect;
evergreen, green foliage;
showy, black fruit

Flower: showy; purple,
lavender or white; spring

Culture: full sun to shade; acid to alkaline
pH; medium salt tolerance; high drought
tolerance; pest sensitive

Notes: forms a solid groundcover in a few
years; mow old, unsightly foliage in late
winter just before new growth appears; one
popular cultivar has variegated foliage that is
damaged by frost

Uses: groundcover, mass planting, edging,
indoors

Liriope muscari 'Evergreen Giant'

(luh-RYE-oh-pee
mus-KAR-ree)

Common name:
'Evergreen Giant' Lilyturf,
'Evergreen Giant' Liriope

Zone: 6a-10b

Size: 1-2' tall and wide;
moderate growth; 18 to 24"
spacing

Form: upright/erect;
evergreen, green foliage;
showy, black fruit

Flower: showy; purple, lavender

Culture: full sun to shade; acid to alkaline
pH; medium salt tolerance; high drought

tolerance; pest sensitive

Notes: adaptable plant for many
landscapes; occasionally used indoors

Uses: groundcover, mass planting, edging

Nephrolepis exaltata (neff-FRAHL-lepp-piss eck-sahl-TAY-tuh)

Common name:
Boston Fern, Sword Fern

Zone: 10a-11

Size: 6"-4' tall depending on cultivar; unlimited spread; fast growth; 24 to 36" spacing

Form: upright/erect; evergreen (south Florida), green foliage

Flower: no flowers

Culture: full sun to shade; tolerates occasional wet soil; acid to slightly alkaline pH; low salt tolerance; medium drought tolerance; pest resistant

Notes: spreads quickly in the garden; killed to the ground by frost but re-emerges in spring; many cultivars available with different leaf form and plant size

Uses: groundcover, mass planting, container, hanging basket, indoors

Ophiopogon japonicus

(oh-fee-oh-POE-gawn juh-PAWN-nick-kuss)

Common name:
Mondo Grass, Dwarf Lilyturf

Zone: 8-10b

Size: 4-8" tall; variable spread; very slow growth; 6 to 12" spacing

Form: upright/erect, spreading; evergreen, dark green foliage

Flower: not showy; white

Culture: partial to full shade; acid to slightly alkaline pH; medium salt tolerance; medium drought tolerance; pest resistant

Notes: plants grow poorly in full sun; dwarf cultivar grows to about 2" tall

Uses: groundcover, mass planting, edging, indoors

G R O U N D C O V E R S

Rhoeo spathacea (REE-oh spath-AY-see-uh)

Common name:
Oyster Plant,
Moses-in-the-Cradle
Zone: 9b-11
Size: 12-18"' tall; variable
spread; slow growth; 18 to
24" spacing
Form: upright/erect;
evergreen, purple and green
foliage
Flower: not showy;
white
Culture: full sun to shade; tolerates
occasional wet soil; acid to alkaline pH;
medium salt tolerance; high drought
tolerance; pest resistant

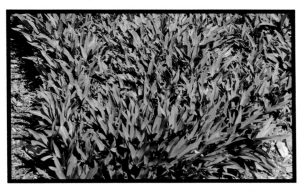

Notes: grows almost anywhere including
the cracks of a garden wall; dwarf cultivar
available
Uses: groundcover, mass planting, container,
indoors, cut foliage, edging

Rumohra adiantiformis

(roo-MOR-ruh
ad-dee-an-tiff-FOR-miss)
Common name:
Leatherleaf Fern
Zone: 9b-11
Size: 1-3' tall; 4-5' wide;
slow growth; 24 to 36"
spacing
Form: upright/erect;
evergreen, green foliage
Flower: no flowers;
plants reproduce by spores
Culture: partial to full shade; acid to
neutral pH; medium salt tolerance; medium
drought tolerance; pest sensitive

Notes: most Leatherleaf Fern grown for
florists comes from central Florida nurseries
Uses: groundcover, mass planting, cut
foliage, edging

Trachelospermum asiaticum

(tray-kell-loe-SPER-mum
ay-shee-AT-tick-kum)

Common name:
Dwarf Jasmine, Small-Leaf
Confederate Jasmine,
Asiatic Jasmine

Zone: 7b-10b

Size: 1' tall; unlimited
spread; fast growth; 24 to
36" spacing

Form: spreading;
evergreen, green foliage

Flower: not showy, not common;
yellowish-white; spring

Culture: full sun to partial shade; acid to
alkaline pH; medium salt tolerance; medium
drought tolerance; pest sensitive

Notes: often chokes out other plants;
regular clipping is required along the edges of
the bed to check aggressive growth; foliage
browns in low 20 degree temperatures; a
variegated cultivar is occasionally seen

Uses: ground cover, cascade effect, bank
stabilization

Tulbaghia violacea (tool-BAIG-ee-uh vye-oh-LAY-see-uh)

Common name:
Society Garlic

Zone: 8a-11

Size: 1-2' tall and wide;
slow growth; 18 to 24"
spacing

Form: upright/erect;
semi-evergreen, green
foliage

Flower: showy; purple,
lavender; spring, summer,
fall

Culture: full sun to partial shade; acid to
alkaline pH; medium salt tolerance; medium
drought tolerance; pest resistant

Notes: plants have strong garlic scent; will
not flower well in shade; variegated form
available

Uses: groundcover, mass planting, edging

Vinca major (VINK-kuh MAY-jer)

Common name: Big Periwinkle, Greater Periwinkle

Zone: 7a-9

Size: 6-12" tall; unlimited spread; moderate growth; 12 to 18" spacing

Form: upright/erect, spreading; evergreen, green foliage

Flower: showy; blue, purple, lavender

Culture: partial to full shade; tolerates occasional wet soil; acid to slightly alkaline pH; low salt tolerance; medium drought tolerance; pest resistant

Notes: forms a fairly dense ground cover in partial shade with flowers scattered through the bed; a variegated cultivar is occasionally available; one of the few flowering ground-covers for the shade; poisonous

Uses: groundcover, mass planting, container, naturalizing; cascade effect

Wedelia trilobata (wee-DEEL-lee-uh try-loe-BAY-tuh)

Common name: Wedelia

Zone: 10a-11

Size: 6-12" tall; unlimited spread; fast growth; 18 to 24" spacing

Form: spreading, upright/erect; evergreen (south Florida) green foliage; brown fruit

Flower: showy; yellow; year-round

Culture: full sun to partial shade; tolerates wet soil; acid to alkaline pH; high salt tolerance; high drought tolerance; pest sensitive

Notes: invades surrounding landscapes and can become a weed; frozen to the ground but comes back in spring in the warmest parts of zones 8b-9b

Uses: groundcover, mass planting, container, hanging basket, cascade effect

PALMS

Many palms are grown in Florida but only about 30 are commonly available in nurseries. Most, including the Date Palms, grow best in well-drained soil. Never plant deeper than the palm was in the nursery, as this shortens their life. Most can be grown in full sun or partial shade, in soil with an acid to slightly alkaline pH. Although many adapt to alkaline soil, typical of south Florida, they look best with regular applications of fertilizer especially formulated for palms. These are usually available at garden centers and sold as 'palm specials' or 'palm fertilizers'. Three applications per year are usually recommended to keep foliage green and plants vigorous.

Many palms are tolerant of drought once they become established. However, during establishment, regular irrigation and fertilizer applications are recommended. Leaves on Sabal Palms are often removed before they reach the planting site. This practice has been shown to improve survival of Sabal Palms that receive little irrigation after planting, but provides little or no benefit to palms receiving irrigation after planting. Some of the oldest leaves on Date Palms, transplanted from a field nursery, are removed to help minimize transplant stress. Leaves do not need to be removed on any palm planted from a container. Green leaves should not be removed from established palms.

Transplanted Date Palms and Sabal Palms often benefit from a preventive pesticide program, until established, to guard against weevil attack. These insects can kill the palm. As with other plants, lethal diseases can enter the trunk if it is injured. Maintain an adequate mulch area around the trunk to keep mowing equipment away. At least one lethal disease (Fusarium wilt) can be spread by pruning a diseased Canary Island Date Palm and then pruning a healthy palm. Be sure to disinfect the pruning tool after pruning susceptible Date Palms.

Acoelorrhaphe wrightii (ah-see-loe-RAY-fee RITE-ee-eye)

Common name: Paurotis Palm

Zone: 9b-11; Florida native

Size: 15-25' tall; 10-15' wide; slow growth; 10-15' spacing

Form: multi-trunk; green foliage; showy, black fruit

Flower: showy; yellow, creamy white

Culture: full sun to partial shade; tolerates wet soil; acid to slightly alkaline pH; medium salt tolerance; medium drought tolerance; pest resistant

Notes: plant forms a dense clump with many stems; one of the few available palms that can grow in wet soil; petioles are armed with sharp teeth; without regular fertilazation, older leaves become chlorotic (loss of green color)

Uses: specimen, planter

Archontophoenix alexandrae

(ar-kawn-toe-FEE-nicks al-leck-SAN-dree)

Common name: Alexandra Palm, King Alexander Palm

Zone: 10b-11

Size: 30-40' tall; 10-15' wide; moderate growth; 10-15' spacing

Form: single trunk; green foliage; showy, bright red fruit

Flower: showy; white

Culture: full sun to partial shade; acid to slightly alkaline pH; low salt tolerance; high drought tolerance; pest resistant

Notes: *A. cunninghamiana* is very similar and is slightly more cold hardy

Uses: specimen, container or planter, street tree, indoors

Bismarckia nobilis (biz-MAR-kee-uh no-BILL-iss)

Common name: Bismarck Palm
Zone: 10a-11
Size: 40-60' tall; 15-20' wide; slow growth; 10-15' spacing
Form: single trunk; blue foliage
Flower: somewhat showy; maroon and white
Culture: full sun to partial shade; acid to slightly alkaline pH; medium salt tolerance; high drought tolerance; pest resistant
Notes: striking blue leaves makes this a popular palm; plant only where huge spread of crown won't be a problem; do not transplant until a trunk forms
Uses: specimen, buffer or median, indoors

Butia capitata (BEW-tee-uh kap-ih-TAY-tuh)

Common name: Pindo Palm, Jelly Palm
Zone: 8-10b
Size: 15-25' tall; 10-15' wide; slow growth; 10-15' spacing
Form: single trunk; silver-blue to green foliage; showy, yellow-orange, edible fruit
Flower: showy; white
Culture: full sun to partial shade; acid to slightly alkaline pH; medium salt tolerance; high drought tolerance; pest sensitive
Notes: fine-textured palm which looks its best in full sun; edible fruit is used for jelly
Uses: street tree, specimen, parking lot buffer strip or median; edible fruit

Caryota spp. (kair-ee-OH-tuh species)

Common name: Fishtail Palm

Zone: 10b-11

Size: 15-25' tall; 10-15' wide; moderate growth; 10' spacing

Form: single or multi-trunk palm; green foliage; red to black fruit

Flower: not showy; white

Culture: full sun to shade; acid to alkaline pH; low salt tolerance; medium drought tolerance; pest resistant

Notes: Fishtail palms are susceptible to lethal yellowing disease; these palms die after flowering in about 20 years; *C. urens* is single-trunked; *C. mitis* is multi-trunked; fruit is an irritant

Uses: indoors, specimen, planter, screen

Chamaedorea erumpens

(kam-mee-DOR-ree-uh ee-RUMP-penz)

Common name: Bamboo Palm

Zone: 10b-11

Size: 4-12' tall; 3-5' wide; moderate growth; 36 to 60" spacing

Form: multi-stemmed; green foliage; black fruit

Flower: not showy; creamy white

Culture: partial to full shade; acid to slightly alkaline pH; low salt tolerance; medium drought tolerance; pest sensitive

Notes: a fine plant for indoor use, frequently seen in homes and malls; frequently gets mites, but is resistant to most pests

Uses: specimen, screen, container, indoors, accent

Chamaedorea microspadix

(kam-mee-DOR-ree-uh
mike-roe-SPAY-dicks)

Common name:
Microspadix Palm, Bamboo
Palm
Zone: 9-11
Size: 8-12' tall; 5-10'
wide; slow growth; 36 to
60" spacing
Form: multi-stemmed;
green foliage; showy, red
fruit on female plants
Flower: showy; yellow
Culture: mostly shaded to full shade; acid
to slightly alkaline pH; low salt tolerance;
medium drought tolerance; pest sensitive
Notes: regular fertilizer application keeps
foliage green; plants have survived, with

some protection, to temperatures as low as 20
degrees
Uses: container, specimen, screen, border,
accent, mass planting, indoors

Chamaerops humilis (kuh-MEE-rops HEW-mih-liss)

Common name: European Fan Palm
Zone: 8a-11
Size: 8-15' tall; 6-10' wide; slow growth; 10'
spacing
Form: typically multi-stemmed, occasionally
solitary; silver/gray to green foliage; brown fruit
Flower: not showy; yellow
Culture: full sun to partial shade; acid to
alkaline pH; medium salt tolerance; high drought
tolerance; pest sensitive
Notes: a great accent plant; relatively low
maintenance compared to other palms; petioles
are armed with sharp teeth
Uses: screen, specimen, planter, border, mass
planting, accent, indoors

Chrysalidocarpus lutescens

(kriss-al-lid-oh-KAR-pus loo-TESS-enz)

Common name: Areca Palm; Butterfly Palm

Zone: 10b-11

Size: 20-30′ tall; 8-10′ wide; fast growth; 6 to 10′ spacing

Form: multi-stemmed; green foliage; yellow to purple/black fruit

Flower: not showy; white

Culture: full sun to partial shade; tolerates occasional wet soil; acid to slightly alkaline pH; medium salt tolerance; high drought tolerance; pest sensitive

Notes: traditionally used as a house plant; requires regular fertilization to keep leaves green

Uses: indoors, screen, specimen, container or planter

Cocos nucifera (KOE-koase noo-SIFF-er-uh)

Common name: Coconut Palm

Zone: 10b-11

Size: 50-80′ tall; 15-25′ wide; moderate growth; 15′ spacing

Form: single trunk; green or greenish-yellow foliage; showy, brown, green or yellow fruit

Flower: somewhat showy; creamy white

Culture: full sun; acid to alkaline pH; excellent salt tolerance; high drought tolerance; pest sensitive

Notes: select only disease resistant plants from reputable nurseries; 'Maypan' and 'Malayan Dwarf' selections are mostly resistant to lethal yellowing disease

Uses: street tree, specimen, seashore palm, shade tree, edible fruit

P A L M S

Cycas revoluta (SYE-kuss rev-voe-LOOT-tuh)

Common name:
King Sago
Zone: 8b-11
Size: 3-10' tall; 4-8' wide;
slow growth; 3-5' spacing
Form: palm-like; green
foliage; showy, red, brown
fruit
Flower: not showy
Culture: full sun to
partial shade; acid to

slightly alkaline pH; medium salt tolerance; high drought tolerance; pest sensitive
Notes: not a true palm; scales and mealy-bugs can infest foliage; foliage turns brown with temperatures close to 20 degrees; manganese deficiency causes foliage

discoloration and distortion; several related cycads (*C. circinalis* and *C. taiwaniana*) also make good landscape plants but they are less cold hardy; poisonous
Uses: specimen, container or planter, border, mass planting, accent, indoors

Howea forsteriana (HOW-ee-uh for-stair-ee-AY-nuh)

Common name: Kentia Palm, Sentry Palm
Zone: 9b-11
Size: 15-25' tall; 6-10' wide; slow growth; 5-10' spacing
Form: single-stem; dark green foliage; yellow, red fruit
Flower: not showy; creamy white
Culture: partial to full shade; acid to slightly alkaline pH; medium salt tolerance; medium drought tolerance; pest sensitive
Notes: one of the most graceful palms for interior use; susceptibility to phytophthora root rot makes this plant best suited for well-drained sites
Uses: indoors, specimen, container or planter

58

Latania spp. (lat-TAY-nee-uh species)

Common name: Latan Palm
Zone: 10b-11
Size: 20-30' tall; 10-12' wide; slow growth; 12-15' spacing
Form: single trunk; silver/gray foliage; greenish-brown fruit
Flower: not showy; yellow, creamy white
Culture: full sun to partial shade; acid to slightly alkaline pH; low to medium salt tolerance; high drought tolerance; pest sensitive
Notes: *L. lontaroides* (Red Latan Palm) and *L. loddigesii* (Blue Latan Palm) are the most common species; both are susceptible to lethal yellowing disease
Uses: specimen, planter

Livistona chinensis (liv-iss-TOE-nuh chih-NEN-sis)

Common name: Chinese Fan Palm
Zone: 9-11
Size: 25-35' tall; 10-12' wide; moderate growth; 10' spacing
Form: single trunk; green foliage; blue, black fruit
Flower: not showy; creamy white
Culture: full sun to partial shade; acid to alkaline pH; medium salt tolerance; high drought tolerance; pest resistant
Notes: tips of leaves droop creating a delicate texture; moderately susceptible to lethal yellowing disease
Uses: indoors, specimen

Neodypsis decaryi (nee-oh-DIP-sis dee-KAR-yi)

Common name: Triangle Palm
Zone: 10b-11
Size: 20-25' tall; 10-15' wide; moderate growth; 10' spacing
Form: single trunk; blue-green foliage; yellow-green fruit
Flower: showy; creamy white
Culture: full sun to partial shade; acid to alkaline pH; low salt tolerance; high drought tolerance; pest resistant
Notes: this palm is distinctly three-sided; makes a nice accent plant, provided there is enough room in the landscape
Uses: buffer, specimen, street tree

Phoenix canariensis (FEE-nicks kan-air-ee-EN-sis)

Common name: Canary Island Date Palm
Zone: 8b-11
Size: 40-60' tall; 20-25' wide; slow growth; 20' spacing
Form: single trunk; green foliage; showy, orange to yellow fruit
Flower: somewhat showy; creamy white
Culture: full sun; acid to alkaline pH; medium salt tolerance; high drought tolerance; pest and disease sensitive
Notes: older leaves often yellow due to magnesium deficiency; watch for butt rot and Fusarium wilt which are lethal; plant only in well-drained soil with the water table well below the surface
Uses: street tree, specimen, parking lot island, buffer or median

Syagrus romanzoffiana (sigh-AY-gruss roe-man-zoff-ee-AY-nuh)

Common name: Queen Palm, Cocos
Plumosa Palm

Zone: 10a-11

Size: 25-40' tall; 15-25' wide; rapid growth; 12-
15' spacing

Form: single trunk; dark green foliage; showy,
orange fruit

Flower: showy; creamy white

Culture: full sun; tolerates occasional wet soil;
acid pH; medium salt tolerance; medium drought
tolerance; pest resistant

Notes: commonly available and inexpensive;
regular applications of manganese help prevent
"Frizzletop," a condition causing small leaves and
poor growth

Uses: specimen

Trachycarpus fortunei (tray-kee-KAR-pus FOR-too-nee-eye)

Common name: Windmill Palm

Zone: 8a-11

Size: 15-25' tall; 6-10' wide; slow growth; 8-10'
spacing

Form: single trunk; green foliage; bluish fruit

Flower: not showy; yellowish-white

Culture: mostly sunny to shade; acid to
alkaline pH; medium salt tolerance; high drought
tolerance; pest sensitive

Notes: great palm for shaded landscapes; enjoys
some shade in the afternoon in summer; watch
for scale infestation

Uses: indoors, on a deck or patio in a planter,
specimen

Thrinax radiata (THRY-nacks ray-dee-AY-tuh)

Common name: Florida Thatch Palm
Zone: 10b-11; Florida native
Size: 15-20' tall; 6-10' wide; slow growth; 10' spacing
Form: single trunk; green foliage; showy, white fruit
Flower: somewhat showy; white
Culture: full sun to partial shade; acid to alkaline pH; high salt tolerance; high drought tolerance; pest resistant
Notes: coarse textured, low maintenance palm for many landscape situations due to its small size
Uses: on a deck or patio in a planter, specimen, buffer or median, street tree

Veitchia merrillii (VEE-chee-uh mer-RILL-ee-eye)

Common name: Christmas Palm, Manila Palm, Adonidia Palm
Zone: 10b-11
Size: 15-25' tall; 8-10' wide; moderate growth; 10' spacing
Form: single trunk; green foliage; very showy, red fruit in winter
Flower: somewhat showy; yellowish-white
Culture: full sun to partial shade; acid to slightly alkaline pH; medium salt tolerance; high drought tolerance; pest resistant
Notes: lethal yellowing disease can kill the palm; enjoys a popularity in malls at present; red fruit presents quite a show
Uses: indoors, specimen, container or planter

Washingtonia robusta (wosh-ing-TOE-nee-uh roe-BUS-tuh)

Common name: Washington Palm, Mexican Fan Palm

Zone: 8-11

Size: 60-90' tall; 10-15' wide; rapid growth; 15' spacing

Form: single trunk; green foliage; black fruit

Flower: showy; creamy white

Culture: full sun to partial shade; acid to alkaline pH; medium salt tolerance; high drought tolerance; pest sensitive

Notes: fast growing palm that quickly outgrows its space in a residential landscape; temperatures in the low 20's burn the foliage but usually do not kill the palm

Uses: street tree, specimen, median strip

Wodyetia bifurcata (wood-yah-TEE-ah bye-fur-CAY-tah)

Common name: Foxtail Palm

Zone: 10a-11

Size: 30' tall; 8-10' wide; fast growth; 10' spacing

Form: single trunk; green foliage; black fruit

Flower: showy; creamy white

Culture: full sun to partial shade; acid to slightly alkaline pH; medium salt tolerance; medium drought tolerance; pest resistant

Notes: a fast growing, delicate palm gaining popularity for residential and commercial landscapes; leaves resemble a fox tail; seems adaptable to a wide range of soil conditions

Uses: street tree, specimen, median strip

SHRUBS

In many ways, shrubs form the walls of our landscape. They help screen undesirable views, form boundaries between residential properties and filter out noise. They help hide an exposed foundation and soften the effects of a tall building corner. Planted in mass along the highway or along an embankment, they reduce soil erosion. They can also provide a year-long flower display if selected thoughtfully.

The biggest mistake people make with shrubs is choosing one that outgrows its allocated space in the landscape. This leads to endless clipping and disfigured plants as the shrub grows too large. To minimize the amount of work in your yard, choose a plant that grows to the size you want. There are many dwarf cultivars of the common large-growing shrubs offered by local nurseries. Ask for them if you do not see them.

To install a group of shrubs in compacted soil, dig up and loosen the soil in the entire area about as deep as the root ball. After watering plants well, remove the containers and slip plants into a hole as deep as the root ball. In all soils, set plants so the top of the root ball is slightly above the surrounding soil. Do not spread soil over the top of the root ball as this will keep roots too dry. Spread a 3-inch-thick layer of organic mulch over the entire area. Maintain the mulch to at least the edge of the plant. Water root balls at least twice each week in spring, summer and early fall, until plants are established. Plants require from 3 months (one gallon size) to one year (7 gallon size) to become established. Plants installed in the winter can be watered once (north Florida) or twice (south Florida) a week. During the establishment period, frequent light applications of water are preferable to infrequent heavy applications.

Abelia x grandiflora (uh-BEEL-lee-uh gran-diff-FLOR-ruh)

Common name:
Glossy Abelia
Zone: 5a-9b
Size: 6-10' tall and wide;
moderate growth; 36 to
60" spacing
Form: vase, round;
evergreen foliage emerges
purple/red and turns
green; tan fruit
Flower: showy; pink;
summer

Culture: full sun to partial shade; acid to
slightly alkaline pH; low salt tolerance;
medium drought tolerance; pest resistant
Notes: flowers nearly year-round in
central Florida, in warm months in the
north; 'Sherwoodii' is smaller like Dwarf
Yaupon Holly; 'Edward Goucher' has
deeper pink flowers
Uses: foundation, border, mass planting,
container or planter, hedge, specimen,
screen, attracts butterflies, cascade effect

Acalypha hispida (ack-kuh-LIFE-fuh HISS-pid-duh)

Common name:
Chenille Plant
Zone: 10b-11
Size: 4-6' tall; 6-8' wide;
fast growth; 36 to 60"
spacing
Form: round; evergreen,
green foliage
Flower: showy and
delicate; red; year-round
Culture: full sun; acid

to slightly alkaline pH; medium salt
tolerance; low drought tolerance; pest
sensitive
Notes: flowers gracefully hang from stems
Uses: container or planter, hedge,
specimen, foundation, border, mass
planting, accent

Acalypha wilkesiana (ack-kuh-LIFE-fuh wilk-see-AY-nuh)

Common name:
Copperleaf, Jacob's Coat
Zone: 10b-11
Size: 8-12' tall; 6-8'
wide; fast growth; 36 to
60" spacing
Form: round,
upright/erect; evergreen,
variegated, purple/red,
green and pink foliage
Flower: not showy; red

Culture: full sun to partial shade; tolerates occasional wet soil; acid to slightly alkaline pH; medium salt tolerance; low drought tolerance; pest sensitive

Notes: grown primarily for its reddish-pink foliage
Uses: foundation, hedge, border, mass planting, container or planter, screen, accent

Acrostichum daneifolium

(ack-roe-STISH-shum
dan-nee-iff-FOLE-lee-um)
Common name:
Leather Fern
Zone 9a-11; Florida native
Size: 4-8' tall; 3-5' wide;
moderate growth; 36 to
60" spacing
Form: upright/erect;
evergreen, green foliage
Flower: ferns produce
spores, not flowers

Culture: partial to full shade; tolerates wet soil; acid to slightly alkaline pH; high salt tolerance; low drought tolerance; pest resistant
Notes: nice plant for a wet spot in a shaded landscape; foliage sometimes discolors in full sun without regular irrigation
Uses: specimen, mass planting, accent, border

S H R U B S

Agave americana (uh-GAH-vee uh-mair-rick-KAY-nuh)

Common name:
Century Plant
Zone: 9a–11
Size: 6–8' tall; 8–10'
wide; slow growth; 8–10'
spacing
Form: round; evergreen,
silver/gray to blue-green
foliage; showy, green,
brown fruit

Flower: showy;
produced on a 20' tall stalk; white;
summer, fall
Culture: full sun to partial shade; acid to
alkaline pH; high salt tolerance; high
drought tolerance; pest resistant
Notes: plant dies after it flowers; allow
plenty of room for this large plant to
spread; leaves eventually reach about 8'
long and have a sharply pointed tip; *A.
angustifolia* is also a nice plant with
narrower foliage
Uses: specimen, border, accent, mass
planting

Allamanda neriifolia (al-luh-MAN-duh neer-ree-iff-FOLE-lee-uh)

Common name:
Bush Allamanda
Zone: 10b–11
Size: 4–6' tall and wide;
moderate growth; 36 to
60" spacing
Form: round, spreading;
evergreen, green foliage;
showy, green then brown
fruit

Flower: showy; yellow;
nearly year-round
Culture: full sun to partial shade; acid to
alkaline pH; medium salt tolerance;
medium drought tolerance; pest resistant
Notes: makes an open hedge; could be
nice when mass planted along highway
interchanges
Uses: specimen, container or planter,
foundation, border

Ardisia escallonioides

(ar-DIZ-zee-uh ess-kal-lawn-nee-OY-deez)

Common name: Marlberry, Marbleberry

Zone: 10a-11; Florida native

Size: 12-20' tall; 6-12' wide; moderate growth; 5-10' spacing

Form: vase, oval; evergreen, green foliage; showy, purple, red fruit

Flower: somewhat showy; white; spring, summer, fall

Culture: full sun to partial shade; acid to alkaline pH; high salt tolerance; medium drought tolerance; pest resistant

Notes: shiny foliage and dense habit makes this a great plant for screens and hedges; can be trained into a small tree

Uses: hedge, specimen, screen, attracts butterflies, border

Berberis thunbergii (BER-ber-riss thun-BER-jee-eye)

Common name: Japanese Barberry

Zone: 4a-9b

Size: 2-8' tall; 4-6' wide; slow growth; 36 to 60" spacing

Form: round; semi-evergreen, green or purple/red foliage; showy, red fruit

Flower: not showy; yellowish-white

Culture: full sun to partial shade; acid to alkaline pH; low salt tolerance; medium drought tolerance; pest resistant

Notes: used most often in north Florida; low maintenance plant; dwarf cultivars are suited for small residential lots; short thorns on branches

Uses: foundation, border, mass planting, groundcover, hedge, edging

S H R U B S

Bougainvillea spp. (boog-inn-VILL-lee-uh species)

Common name:
Bougainvillea
Zone: 9b-11
Size: variable height, usually less than 15'; 15-40' wide; fast growth; 36 to 60" spacing
Form: spreading, irregular; semi-evergreen, green foliage
Flower: showy; orange,

purple, red, lavender, yellow; periodically throughout the year
Culture: full sun for best flowering; acid to slightly alkaline pH; high salt tolerance; high drought tolerance; pest sensitive
Notes: cultivars available with variegated foliage, various flower colors and plant

sizes; spiny stems warrant care when pruning these plants
Uses: bonsai, specimen, hedge, container or planter, mass planting, groundcover, trained as a standard, espalier, hanging basket, cascade effect, vine

Buddleia spp. (bud-LEE-uh species)

Common name:
Butterfly-Bush
Zone: 6a-10b
Size: 6-12' tall and wide; fast growth; 5' spacing
Form: round; semi-evergreen, blue-green to green foliage
Flower: showy; lavender, white, purple or pink; throughout the warm months

Culture: full sun; tolerates occasional wet soil; acid to alkaline pH; medium salt tolerance; medium drought tolerance; pest sensitive

Notes: holds leaves into winter
Uses: bonsai, container or planter, trained as a standard, accent, border, attracts butterflies

Buxus microphylla (BUCK-suss mike-roe-FILL-luh)

Common name:
Littleleaf Boxwood,
Littleleaf Box
Zone: 6a-10a
Size: 3-6' tall and wide;
slow growth; 24 to 36"
spacing
Form: round; evergreen,
green foliage
Flower: not showy;
green

Culture: full sun to partial shade; acid to slightly alkaline pH; low salt tolerance; medium drought tolerance; pest sensitive
Notes: makes a great, small hedge; recovers slowly when damaged, due to its slow growth; many cultivars are available; poisonous
Uses: bonsai, border, edging, foundation, excellent hedge

Caesalpinia pulcherrima

(sez-al-PIN-nee-uh
pul-KAIR-rim-muh)
Common name:
Dwarf Poinciana,
Barbados Flowerfence
Zone: 9-11
Size: 8-12' tall and wide;
fast growth; 8' spacing
Form: round; evergreen,
green foliage; brown fruit
Flower: showy; red,

yellow or orange; in warm months
Culture: full sun to partial shade; acid to alkaline pH; medium salt tolerance; high drought tolerance; pest sensitive
Notes: striking flowers fill the canopy most of the year; watch for thorns along the stems; poisonous
Uses: specimen, container, shrub, border

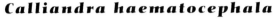

Calliandra haematocephala

(kal-lee-AN-druh hee-
mat-toe-SEFF-fuh-luh)

Common name:
Powder Puff

Zone: 10a-11

Size: 12-15' tall and
wide; fast growth; 6-10'
spacing

Form: vase, round;
evergreen, green foliage

Flower: showy; red;
nearly year-round

Culture: full sun to partial shade; acid to
slightly alkaline pH; low salt tolerance; high
drought tolerance; pest sensitive

Notes: will grow in zone 9a but is killed

to the ground every few years; a white
form is available at some nurseries

Uses: hedge, specimen, container or
planter, trained as a standard, espalier,
buffer or median

Camellia spp. (kuh-MEEL-lee-uh species)

Common name:
Camellia

Zone: 7a-9b

Size: 7-12' tall; 5-10'
wide; slow growth; 36 to
60" spacing

Form: oval, upright;
evergreen, green foliage

Flower: showy; white,
orange, pink, red, yellow
or lavender; fall through
early spring

Culture: full sun to partial shade
depending on cultivar; acid pH; low salt
tolerance; low drought tolerance; pest
sensitive

Notes: hundreds of cultivars are available
in an endless variety of colors

Uses: bonsai, screen, border, specimen,
container or planter, espalier, foundation

Carissa macrocarpa (grandiflora)

(kuh-RISS-suh mack-roe-CAR-puh)

Common name: Natal Plum, Common Carissa

Zone: 9b-11

Size: 6-10' tall; 4-10' wide; moderate growth; 36 to 60" spacing

Form: round, spreading; evergreen, green foliage; showy, edible, red fruit

Flower: showy; pure white; spring, summer, fall

Culture: full sun to partial shade; acid to alkaline pH; high salt tolerance; high drought tolerance; pest sensitive

Notes: dwarf cultivars make good groundcovers and container plants

Uses: dune stabilization, bonsai, foundation, screen, border, mass planting, container or planter, fruit, espalier, groundcover, hedge

Cassia alata (KASS-see-uh uh-LAY-tuh)

Common name: Candlebush

Zone: 10a-11

Size: 10-15' tall and wide; fast growth; 8-10' spacing

Form: oval; evergreen, green foliage

Flower: very showy; yellow; summer and fall

Culture: full sun; acid to slightly alkaline pH; medium salt tolerance; medium drought tolerance; pest resistant

Notes: large, upright flowers put on a

spectacular display

Uses: specimen, container or planter, trained as a standard, buffer or median

S H R U B S

Cassia bicapsularis (KASS-see-uh bye-kap-soo-LAIR-riss)

Common name:
Cassia Shrub
Zone: 10a-11
Size: 8-12' tall and wide;
moderate growth; 6-10'
spacing
Form: floppy, rounded,
vase; semi-evergreen,
green foliage; brown fruit
Flower: showy; yellow;
fall

Culture: full sun to partial shade; acid to slightly alkaline pH; medium salt tolerance; medium drought tolerance; pest sensitive

Notes: most plants fall over unless they are staked or maintained by clipping; foliage and flower buds are sometimes chewed by caterpillars, which reduces flower display; poisonous

Uses: specimen, container or planter, buffer or median

Chrysobalanus icaco (kriss-soe-ball-LAY-nuss eye-KAY-koe)

Common name: Cocoplum
Zone: 10b-11; Florida native
Size: 10-20' tall; 10-15' wide; moderate
growth; 36 to 60" spacing
Form: round, vase; evergreen, green foliage;
showy, purple fruit
Flower: not showy; white
Culture: full sun to partial shade; acid to
alkaline pH; high salt tolerance; medium
drought tolerance; pest resistant
Notes: commonly used as a hedge in south
Florida; can be trained into a small, multi-
stemmed tree; red-tipped form has purple-red
new growth
Uses: foundation, screen, fruit, container or
planter, trained as a standard, excellent hedge,
parking lot island, border

Codiaeum variegatum (koe-dih-EE-um vair-ree-egg-GAY-tum)

Common name:
Croton
Zone: 10b-11
Size: 3-8' tall; 3-6' wide;
slow growth; 24 to 36"
spacing
Form: upright/erect,
oval; evergreen,
variegated, yellow, purple
and red foliage
Flower: not showy;
white

Culture: full sun to partial shade; acid to alkaline pH; medium salt tolerance; high drought tolerance; pest sensitive

Notes: plants vary in leaf size, shape, color and variegation pattern

Uses: foundation, hedge, border, mass planting, container or planter, indoors, accent, screen

Dracaena marginata (druh-SEEN-nuh mar-jin-NAY-tuh)

Common name: Red-Edged Dracaena, Madagascar Dragon-Tree
Zone: 10b-11
Size: 8-15' tall; 3-8' wide; slow growth; 36 to 60" spacing
Form: upright/erect; evergreen, striped, green and purplish-red foliage
Flower: not showy; white
Culture: full sun to partial shade; acid to slightly alkaline pH; low salt tolerance; high drought tolerance; pest resistant
Notes: commonly used as a house plant but grows nicely in the garden as well; 'Tricolor' has foliage edged in red and is commonly used indoors
Uses: specimen, container or planter, indoors, accent

Eugenia uniflora (yoo-JEEN-nee-uh yoo-niff-FLOR-ruh)

Common name:
Surinam Cherry

Zone: 10a-11

Size: 8-20' tall; 6-15'
wide; moderate growth;
36 to 60" spacing

Form: vase, oval;
evergreen, foliage emerges
red and turns green;
showy, reddish-orange,
edible fruit

Flower: showy but small; white; spring

Culture: full sun to partial shade; acid to
alkaline pH; medium salt tolerance;
medium drought tolerance; pest sensitive

Notes: this commonly used hedge plant
can also be trained into a small multi-
stemmed tree; bark is smooth and showy;
self-seeds and can become weedy

Uses: screen, fruit, hedge, container or
planter, trained as a standard, buffer or
median, border

Fatsia japonica (FAT-see-uh juh-PAWN-nick-kuh)

Common name:
Fatsia

Zone: 8a-11

Size: 5-8' tall; 4-10'
wide; moderate growth;
36 to 60" spacing

Form: upright/erect,
round; evergreen, green
foliage; showy, green fruit
maturing to black

Flower: showy; white;
fall

Culture: partial to full shade; acid to
slightly alkaline pH; medium salt tolerance;
medium drought tolerance; pest sensitive

Notes: plants are best suited for total
shade; lends a tropical effect to the
landscape because of the large leaves

Uses: border, mass planting, specimen,
container or planter, indoors, accent,
foundation

Feijoa sellowiana (fay-JOE-uh sell-loe-wee-AY-nuh)

Common name:
Pineapple Guava, Feijoa
Zone: 9-11
Size: 10-15' tall and
wide; moderate growth;
3-5' spacing as a hedge
Form: spreading,
upright/erect, round;
green foliage; showy,
green, yellow fruit
Flower: showy; white
and red; spring

Culture: full sun to partial shade; acid to
slightly alkaline pH; medium salt tolerance;
high drought tolerance; pest resistant

Notes: although commonly used as a
hedge, Pineapple Guava makes a wonderful
small tree with attractive, exfoliating bark
Uses: specimen, screen, hedge, fruit

Forestiera segregata (far-ress-TEER-ruh seg-ruh-GAY-tuh)

Common name:
Florida Privet, Wild Olive,
Ink-Bush
Zone: 8b-11; Florida
native
Size: 10-15' tall; 5-10'
wide; moderate growth;
4-6' spacing as a hedge
Form: vase, oval;
evergreen, green foliage;
showy, bluish-purple fruit

Flower: not showy; greenish-yellow
Culture: full sun to partial shade;
tolerates wet soil; acid to alkaline pH; high
salt tolerance; high drought tolerance; pest
resistant

Notes: because of the small foliage, Privet
makes a great hedge or screen; plants can
be trained into a small tree
Uses: container or planter, excellent hedge,
espalier, specimen, screen, attracts butterflies

Galphimia glauca (gal-FIM-mee-uh GLOCK-kuh)

Common name:
Thryallis, Rain-of-Gold

Zone: 9-11

Size: 5-9' tall; 4-6' wide;
moderate growth; 36 to
60" spacing

Form: round, oval;
evergreen, green foliage;
green fruit

Flower: showy; yellow;
nearly year-round in

south Florida, warm months in central
Florida

Culture: full sun; acid to slightly alkaline
pH; medium salt tolerance; medium
drought tolerance; pest resistant

Notes: a delicate, flowering shrub, best
suited for a sunny spot in the garden

Uses: hedge, border, mass planting,
specimen, container or planter

Gamolepis chrysanthemoides

(gam-moe-LEP-piss
kriss-santh-ee-MOY-deez)

Common name:
African Bush-Daisy,
Daisy-Bush

Zone: 9-11

Size: 2-4' tall; 3-4' wide;
moderate growth; 24 to
36" spacing

Form: round; green
foliage

Flower: showy; yellow; in warm months

Culture: full sun; acid to slightly alkaline
pH; low salt tolerance; medium drought
tolerance; pest resistant

Notes: provide full sun and good air
circulation for best growth; evergreen in

south Florida; killed to the ground at 20
degrees but re-emerges in spring

Uses: mass planting, specimen, border,
container or planter, foundation, attracts
butterflies

Gardenia jasminoides (gar-DEEN-nee-uh jass-min-NOY-deez)

Common name:
Gardenia, Cape-Jasmine
Zone: 8a–10b
Size: 4-8' tall and wide; moderate growth; 5' spacing
Form: round; evergreen, green foliage; orange fruit
Flower: showy and very fragrant; white; spring

Culture: full sun to shade; acid pH; low salt tolerance; low drought tolerance; pest sensitive
Notes: scales commonly infest foliage and reduce vigor; regular applications of fertilizer high in iron help keep foliage green
Uses: bonsai, screen, hedge, border, mass planting, specimen, container or planter, cut flowers

Hamelia patens (huh-MEEL-lee-uh PAY-tenz)

Common name:
Firebush, Scarletbush
Zone: 10a–11; Florida native
Size: 6-12' tall; 5-8' wide; fast growth; 36 to 60" spacing
Form: round, spreading; evergreen, green foliage; showy, black fruit
Flower: showy; orange-red; in warm months

Culture: full sun to shade; tolerates occasional wet soil; acid to alkaline pH; medium salt tolerance; medium to high drought tolerance; pest sensitive
Notes: an excellent plant for any landscape; grown as a perennial in north Florida
Uses: hedge, specimen, accent, screen, border, mass planting, attracts butterflies and hummingbirds

Hibiscus rosa-sinensis (hye-BISS-kuss roe-zuh-sye-NEN-sis)

Common name:
Tropical Hibiscus, Chinese Hibiscus
Zone: 10a-11
Size: 7-12' tall and wide; fast growth; 36 to 60" spacing as a hedge
Form: oval, vase; evergreen, green foliage
Flower: showy; orange, red, yellow, pink, salmon; year-round

Culture: full sun to partial shade; acid to slightly alkaline pH; medium salt tolerance; low drought tolerance; pest sensitive
Notes: scales and aphids occasionally infest foliage; root nematodes severely weaken plants; cultivars with variegated foliage are rather striking
Uses: screen, hedge, border, mass planting, specimen, container or planter, foundation, trained as a standard, espalier, accent, attracts butterflies and hummingbirds

Hibiscus syriacus (hye-BISS-kuss seer-ree-AY-kuss)

Common name:
Rose-of-Sharon, Shrub-Althea
Zone: 5b-9a
Size: 8-12' tall; 6-10' wide; slow growth; 6-8' spacing
Form: upright/erect; deciduous, green foliage; brown fruit
Flower: showy; red, pink, white, purple, blue or lavender; summer, fall

Culture: full sun to partial shade; tolerates occasional wet soil; acid pH; low salt tolerance; low drought tolerance; pest sensitive
Notes: nice plant for accenting a building entrance or small garden; flowers well in partial shade
Uses: specimen, container or planter, trained as a standard

Hydrangea macrophylla

(hye-DRAN-jee-uh
mack-roe-FILL-luh)

Common name:
Bigleaf Hydrangea
Zone: 5b-9a
Size: 6-10' tall; 6-10'
wide; moderate growth;
36 to 60" spacing
Form: round;
deciduous, green foliage;
showy and persistent,
brown fruit

Flower: showy; blue, pink, white, red,
lavender; summer
Culture: nearly full sun to partial shade;
tolerates occasional wet soil; acid to slightly
alkaline pH; low salt tolerance; low drought
tolerance; pest sensitive

Notes: cultivars are available in a variety
of flower colors and with variegated
foliage; if pruning is needed, do it
immediately after flowering to avoid cutting
off next year's flower buds
Uses: border, mass planting, foundation,
specimen, accent, cut flowers

Ilex cornuta 'Burfordii Nana' (EYE-lecks kor-NOO-tuh)

Common name:
Dwarf Burford Holly
Zone: 7a-9b
Size: 8-12' tall; 6-10'
wide; moderate growth;
36 to 60" spacing
Form: round; evergreen,
green foliage
Flower: not showy;
white
Culture: full sun to

partial shade; acid to slightly alkaline pH;
low salt tolerance; medium drought
tolerance; pest sensitive
Notes: spiny foliage makes this a good

barrier plant; scales can infest the foliage
Uses: foundation, hedge, border, mass
planting, cut foliage; attracts bees

S   H   R   U   B   S

Ilex cornuta 'Rotunda' (EYE-lecks kor-NOO-tuh)

Common name:
Dwarf Chinese Holly
Zone: 7a-9b
Size: 4-8' tall; 6-8' wide;
slow growth; 36 to 60"
spacing
Form: round; evergreen,
green foliage
Flower: not showy;
white
Culture: full sun to

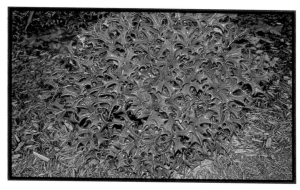

partial shade; acid to slightly alkaline pH;
low salt tolerance; medium drought
tolerance; pest sensitive
Notes: spiny foliage makes this a good

barrier plant
Uses: foundation, border, mass planting,
cut foliage

Ilex crenata (EYE-lecks kren-NAY-tuh)

Common name:
Japanese Holly
Zone: 6-9
Size: 6-10' tall; 5-8'
wide; slow growth; 36 to
60" spacing
Form: round; evergreen,
green foliage
Flower: not showy;
greenish-white
Culture: full sun to

partial shade; acid to slightly alkaline pH;
low salt tolerance; low drought tolerance;
pest sensitive
Notes: traditional hedge plant with darker

green foliage than Boxwood
Uses: foundation, screen, mass planting,
container or planter, excellent hedge, border

85

Ilex vomitoria 'Schellings Dwarf'

(EYE-lecks
vom-mit-TOR-ree-uh)

Common name:
'Schellings Dwarf' Holly
Zone: 7–10; Florida
native
Size: 4–7' tall; 6–10'
wide; slow growth; 36 to
60" spacing
Form: round; evergreen;
green foliage; no fruit

Flower: not showy; white
Culture: full sun to partial shade; tolerates wet soil; acid to slightly alkaline pH; high salt tolerance; high drought tolerance; pest sensitive
Notes: plants grow taller without pruning; used mostly in mass plantings; a serious twig disease can spread quickly on pruning shears; leaf miners tunnel through leaves
Uses: dune stabilization, bonsai, foundation, mass planting, container or planter, hedge, topiary

Illicium floridanum (ill-LISS-see-um flor-rid-DAY-num)

Common name:
Florida Anise Tree,
Florida Anise
Zone: 7b–10a; Florida
native
Size: 10–15' tall; 6–10'
wide; moderate growth;
5–8' spacing
Form: oval; evergreen,
green foliage; green fruit
Flower: showy; purple-

red; spring and summer
Culture: full sun to partial shade; acid to slightly alkaline pH; low salt tolerance; medium drought tolerance; pest sensitive
Notes: dense plant nicely suited for a screen; ambrosia beetles can kill branch tips
Uses: specimen, container or planter, hedge, espalier, screen, foundation, border

S H R U B S

Illicium parviflorum (ill-LISS-see-um par-viff-FLOR-rum)

Common name:
Anise
Zone: 7b-10a; Florida native
Size: 15-20' tall; 10-15' wide; moderate growth; 5-10' spacing
Form: oval; evergreen, green foliage; green fruit
Flower: somewhat showy; whitish-yellow; summer

Culture: full sun to partial shade; acid to slightly alkaline pH; low salt tolerance; medium to high drought tolerance; pest sensitive
Notes: a large plant suited for screening; suckers from the base and roots form a dense thicket; responds well to clipping; can be pruned into a small tree
Uses: planter, hedge, espalier, screen, foundation, border

Ixora coccinea (ick-SOR-ruh kock-SIN-nee-uh)

Common name:
Ixora, Flame of the Woods
Zone: 10a-11
Size: 10-15' tall; 4-10' wide; slow growth; 36 to 60" spacing
Form: upright/erect, oval; evergreen, green foliage
Flower: showy; orange, red, yellow, pink or white; nearly year-round

Culture: full sun to partial shade; acid pH; medium salt tolerance; medium drought tolerance; pest sensitive
Notes: regular applications of fertilizer (including minor elements) are recommended to keep foliage green; best to keep plants away from foundations and sidewalks where soil pH is high; dwarf cultivars make good landscape plants
Uses: screen, border, container or planter, hanging basket, excellent hedge, accent, attracts butterflies

Jasminum multiflorum (JASS-min-num mul-tiff-FLOR-rum)

Common name:
Downy Jasmine
Zone: 9b-11
Size: 5-10' tall and wide;
fast growth; 36 to 60"
spacing as a hedge
Form: spreading, round,
weeping; evergreen, green
foliage
Flower: showy; white;
nearly year-round

Culture: full sun to partial shade; acid to alkaline pH; low salt tolerance; medium drought tolerance; pest sensitive
Notes: forms an open, spreading mass of foliage with small, bright white flowers; best for large landscapes with plenty of room to spread; can be clipped as a hedge
Uses: foundation, mass planting, border, hedge, cascade effect

Juniperus chinensis 'Blue Vase'

(joo-NIP-per-russ
chin-NEN-sis)
Common name:
'Blue Vase' Juniper
Zone: 5-10b
Size: 10-12' tall; 6-10'
wide; moderate growth;
4-8' spacing
Form: upright, rounded;
evergreen, blue foliage;
showy blue fruit
Flower: not showy
Culture: full sun to partial shade; acid to alkaline pH; medium salt tolerance; high drought tolerance; pest sensitive
Notes: nice accent or screen when planted in the full sun
Uses: specimen, screen, container or planter, buffer or median

Juniperus chinensis 'Torulosa'

(joo-NIP-per-russ chin-NEN-sis)

Common name: 'Torulosa' Juniper
Zone: 5-10b
Size: 10-15' tall; 6-10' wide; moderate growth;
6-10' spacing
Form: twisted pyramid, upright/erect;
evergreen, green foliage; showy blue fruit
Flower: not showy
Culture: full sun to partial shade; acid to
alkaline pH; medium salt tolerance; high
drought tolerance; pest sensitive
Notes: nice accent or screen when planted in
full sun; the variegated cultivar has white
foliage interspersed with green
Uses: specimen, screen, container or planter,
espalier, buffer or median

Ligustrum japonicum (lig-GUS-trum juh-PAWN-nick-kum)

Common name:
Japanese Privet, Wax-Leaf
Privet
Zone: 7-10b
Size: 8-12' tall; 15-25'
wide; moderate growth;
4-10' spacing as a hedge
Form: vase, round,
spreading; evergreen,
green foliage; bluish-
purple fruit

Flower: showy; white; summer
Culture: full sun to partial shade; acid to
slightly alkaline pH; medium salt tolerance;
high drought tolerance; pest sensitive
Notes: commonly used as a hedge, but
thins at the bottom unless in the full sun;
makes a nice multi-stemmed small tree;

dwarf cultivars are becoming more
available; plants with variegated foliage are
occasionally offered by nurseries
Uses: screen, specimen, container or
planter, trained as a standard, buffer or
median

Ligustrum sinense 'Variegatum'

(lig-GUS-strum
sye-NEN-see)
Common name:
Variegated Chinese Privet
Zone: 7-10b
Size: 10-20' tall; 8-15'
wide; moderate growth;
36 to 60" spacing as a
hedge
Form: vase, round;
evergreen, green and

white/yellow variegated foliage; black fruit
Flower: showy; white; summer
Culture: full sun to partial shade; acid to
alkaline pH; low salt tolerance; medium
drought tolerance; pest resistant
Notes: quickly outgrows its space in a
residential landscape; foliage often reverts
to green as plants age; has escaped
cultivation in the Panhandle, becoming a
noxious weed
Uses: planter, trained as a standard, hedge,
specimen, border, mass planting, screen

Mahonia fortunei (mah-HOE-nee-uh for-TOON-nee-eye)

Common name: Fortune's Mahonia
Zone: 8-9
Size: 3-4' tall and wide; slow growth; 24 to
36" spacing
Form: upright/erect, round; evergreen, green
foliage; blue, black fruit
Flower: showy; yellow; spring
Culture: partial to full shade; acid to slightly
alkaline pH; medium salt tolerance; medium
drought tolerance; pest resistant
Notes: small, low maintenance plant well
suited for along a foundation on the north or
east side of a building; wonderful shade
tolerance; new foliage emerges red; stems flop
over as plants grow
Uses: foundation, border, mass planting,
specimen, accent

Murraya paniculata (mer-RAY-yuh pan-nick-yoo-LAY-tuh)

Common name:
Orange Jasmine, Chalcas

Zone: 9-11

Size: 8-12' tall; 8-15'
wide; slow growth; 36 to
60" spacing as a hedge

Form: vase, round;
evergreen, green foliage;
showy, red fruit

Flower: showy and
fragrant; white; summer,
spring

Culture: full sun to partial shade; acid to
alkaline pH; medium salt tolerance; high
drought tolerance; pest sensitive

Notes: although used nearly exclusively
as a hedge, twisted trunks make this an
outstanding candidate for growing as a
multi-stemmed small tree

Uses: foundation, screen, border,
specimen, container or planter, excellent
hedge

Myrica cerifera (MEER-rick-kuh ser-RIFF-fer-ruh)

Common name:
Southern Wax Myrtle,
Southern Bayberry

Zone: 7b-11; Florida
native

Size: 15-25' tall; 20-25'
wide; fast growth; 6-10'
spacing

Form: vase, round;
evergreen, fragrant, green
foliage; blue fruit on
female plants

Flower: not showy; green

Culture: full sun to partial shade;
tolerates wet soil; acid to alkaline pH;
medium salt tolerance; medium drought
tolerance; pest sensitive

Notes: since roots fix nitrogen, little if any
fertilizer is required; trunk disease often
shortens its life

Uses: screen, hedge, specimen, planter,
buffer or median

91

Nandina domestica (nan-DEE-nuh doe-MESS-stick-kuh)

Common name:
Nandina, Heavenly
Bamboo
Zone: 7-10b
Size: 5-8' tall; 2-3' wide;
moderate growth; 24 to
36" spacing
Form: upright/erect;
evergreen, green or
purple/red foliage; showy,
red fruit in fall

Flower: showy; white; spring
Culture: full sun to partial shade; acid to slightly alkaline pH; low salt tolerance; medium drought tolerance; pest sensitive
Notes: dwarf cultivars, some with red fall color are becoming popular; to reduce height on a large plant, prune tallest one-third of stems back to 6" long each year
Uses: screen, border, specimen, container or planter, mass planting, accent

Nerium oleander 'Petite Pink'

(NEER-ree-um
ole-lee-AN-der)
Common name:
Dwarf Oleander, 'Petite
Pink' Oleander
Zone: 8-11
Size: 4-6' tall; 5-8' wide;
moderate growth; 36 to
60" spacing
Form: round; evergreen,
green foliage

Flower: showy; pink; nearly year-round
Culture: full sun to partial shade; acid to alkaline pH; high salt tolerance; high drought tolerance; pest sensitive
Notes: this is one of the more common dwarf cultivars; the species is popular as a tall screen; species has white, pink, red or lavender flowers; poisonous
Uses: container or planter, hedge, foundation, border, mass planting

Osmanthus fragrans (oz-MANTH-us FRAY-grunz)

Common name: Sweet Osmanthus
Zone: 7b-9b
Size: 15-30' tall; 15-20' wide; slow growth; 5-10' spacing
Form: upright/erect, then oval; evergreen, green foliage; blue-black fruit, not common
Flower: very fragrant, somewhat showy; creamy-white; fall, winter, spring
Culture: full sun to partial shade; acid pH; low salt tolerance; medium drought tolerance; pest sensitive
Notes: one of the sweetest smelling flowers for Florida landscapes; plants start out with a narrow habit but spread as branches droop to the ground
Uses: hedge, screen, fragrance

Philodendron selloum (fill-loe-DEN-drun sell-LOE-um)

Common name: Selloum
Zone: 9a-11
Size: 6-12' tall; 10-15' wide; fast growth; 5-8' spacing
Form: round; evergreen, green foliage; green fruit
Flower: not showy; green
Culture: full sun to

shade; tolerates occasional wet soil; acid to slightly alkaline pH; low salt tolerance; medium drought tolerance; pest sensitive
Notes: foliage burns with temperatures in the mid to upper 20's; leave plenty of room for this large plant
Uses: border, mass planting, specimen, container or planter, foundation, accent, indoors

Philodendron 'Xanadu' (fill-loe-DEN-drun)

Common name: Philodendron

Zone: 10a-11

Size: 2-3' tall and wide; slow growth; 3-4' spacing

Form: round; evergreen, green foliage

Flower: not showy; green

Culture: full sun to shade; tolerates occasional

wet soil; acid to slightly alkaline pH; low salt tolerance; medium drought tolerance; pest sensitive

Notes: nice plant for a shaded or partially shaded garden

Uses: border, mass planting, specimen, container or planter, foundation, accent, indoors, groundcover

Photinia x fraseri (foe-TIN-nee-uh x FRAY-zer-rye)

Common name: Fraser Photinia, Redtip Photinia

Zone: 7b-9b

Size: 12-18' tall; 8-12' wide; moderate growth; 3-10' spacing as a hedge

Form: upright/erect, oval; evergreen, new foliage is red; orange-red fruit

Flower: showy; white; spring

Culture: full sun; acid to slightly alkaline pH; low salt tolerance; medium drought tolerance; pest sensitive

Notes: grow in full sun to avoid serious leaf spot disease; can be trained into a nice, small tree

Uses: sidewalk cutout, hedge, screen, container or planter, trained as a standard, buffer or median

Pittosporum tobira 'Variegata'

(pit-tuss-SPOR-rum
toe-BYE-ruh)

Common name:
Variegated Pittosporum

Zone: 8-11

Size: 8-12' tall; 12-18'
wide; moderate growth;
36 to 60" spacing

Form: round, vase;
evergreen, green,
variegated foliage; red fruit

Flower: showy and fragrant; white;
spring

Culture: full sun to partial shade; acid to
alkaline pH; high salt tolerance; medium
drought tolerance; pest sensitive

Notes: this is the variegated version of
the green-leaved Pittosporum; be sure to
plant in soil with good drainage because
roots rot in wet soil; watch for scale
infestation; does best in north and central
Florida

Uses: screen, hedge, border, mass planting,
container or planter, trained as a standard

Platycladus orientalis (platt-tick-KLAY-dus or-ree-en-TAY-liss)

Common name:
Arborvitae

Zone: 6a-10b

Size: 12-15' tall and
wide; moderate growth;
5-10' spacing

Form: pyramidal, oval;
evergreen, green foliage;
brown fruit

Flower: not showy

Culture: full sun to

partial shade; acid to slightly alkaline pH;
low salt tolerance; medium drought
tolerance; pest sensitive

Notes: commonly planted for decades as
a standard landscape plant; can be clipped
into a hedge; often seen in old landscapes
as a small tree with lower branches
removed

Uses: specimen, screen, buffer or median

Plumbago auriculata (plum-BAY-go ah-rick-yoo-LAY-tuh)

Common name:
Plumbago, Cape
Plumbago, Sky Flower
Zone: 9-11
Size: 6-10' tall; 8-10'
wide; fast growth; 36 to
60" spacing
Form: spreading, round;
nearly evergreen, green
foliage
Flower: showy;
whitish-blue; warm months

Culture: full sun to partial shade; acid to slightly alkaline pH; medium salt tolerance; medium drought tolerance; pest sensitive
Notes: killed to the ground in mid-20 degree temperatures, but comes back from the roots; one of the few shrubs with blue flowers; a form with deeper blue flowers is available
Uses: foundation, border, mass planting, container or planter, hedge

Polyscias spp. (poe-LISS-see-us species)

Common name: Aralia
Zone: 10b-11
Size: 6-10' tall; 2-4' wide; slow growth; 24 to 36" spacing
Form: upright/erect, round; evergreen, green foliage
Flower: not showy; white
Culture: full sun to shade; tolerates occasional wet soil; acid to slightly alkaline pH; medium salt tolerance; high drought tolerance; pest sensitive
Notes: several species are available, most with an upright growth habit; many are suited for indoor use
Uses: container or planter, hedge, specimen, foundation, border, accent, cut foliage, indoors

Psychotria nervosa (sye-koe-TREE-yuh ner-VOE-suh)

Common name:
Wild Coffee
Zone: 10b-11; Florida native
Size: 4-10' tall and wide; moderate growth; 36 to 60" spacing
Form: oval to round; evergreen, green, glossy foliage; showy, red fruit
Flower: somewhat showy; white; spring, summer
Culture: full sun to shade; acid to alkaline pH; medium salt tolerance; medium drought tolerance; pest resistant
Notes: beautiful native plant that does best in partial to full shade; needs a lot of water in full sun; keep away from windows due to its large size
Uses: container or planter, specimen, hedge, espalier, foundation, border, mass planting

Raphiolepis indica (raff-fee-oh-LEPP-piss IN-dick-kuh)

Common name:
Indian Hawthorn
Zone: 8a-11
Size: 3-7' tall; 6-10' wide; slow growth; 36 to 60" spacing
Form: round, spreading; evergreen, green foliage; showy, purple to blue fruit
Flower: showy; white, pink; spring

Culture: full sun to partial shade; acid to alkaline pH; medium salt tolerance; medium drought tolerance; disease sensitive
Notes: some newer cultivars are reportedly more resistant to leaf spot disease; white-flowered cultivars may be less sensitive to disease; plant in full sun to minimize leaf spot; leaf spot is less of a problem along the coast
Uses: foundation, border, mass planting, container or planter, groundcover

97

Raphiolepis umbellata (raff-fee-OH-lepp-piss um-bell-LAY-tuh)

Common name: Round-Leaf Hawthorn, Yedda Hawthorn

Zone: 8a–10b

Size: 8-12' tall, 6-10' wide; moderate growth; 5-8' spacing

Form: round; evergreen, green foliage; purple fruit

Flower: showy; white or pink; spring

Culture: full sun to partial shade; acid to alkaline pH; medium salt tolerance; medium drought tolerance; disease sensitive

Notes: makes a small, multi-stemmed tree with some training

Uses: screen, border, hedge, specimen, container or planter, trained as a standard, buffer or median

Rhododendron x 'George Taber' (roe-duh-DEN-drun)

Common name: 'George Taber' Azalea

Zone: 8a–10b

Size: 10-12' tall; 8-10' wide; slow growth; 5-6' spacing

Form: round; green foliage; brown fruit

Flower: showy; pink; winter, spring

Culture: partial shade; acid pH; low salt tolerance; low drought tolerance; pest sensitive

Notes: azaleas are available with a variety of flower colors including red, white, salmon, purple and lavender; height ranges from 2-10' tall; plants grow poorly in full shade; flowers on some hybrids, such as 'Fashion', last several months

Uses: border, mass planting, specimen, attracts butterflies, foundation

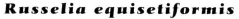

Russelia equisetiformis

(russ-SEEL-lee-uh
eck-kwiss-see-tiff-
FOR-miss)

Common name:
Firecracker Plant

Zone: 9b-11

Size: 3-5' tall; 6-12'
wide; moderate growth;
36 to 60" spacing

Form: round, weeping;
semi-evergreen, green
foliage

Flower: showy; red; in warm months

Culture: full sun; acid to alkaline pH;
high salt tolerance; high drought tolerance;
pest sensitive

Notes: fine-textured plant for a large
landscape

Uses: container or planter, specimen,
foundation, border, mass planting, cascade
effect, accent

Scaevola frutescens (see-VOLE-luh froo-TESS-senz)

Common name:
Scaevola, Beach Naupaka

Zone: 10a-11

Size: 3-10' tall; 3-6'
wide; moderate growth;
36 to 60" spacing

Form: round; soft,
evergreen, green foliage;
showy, white fruit

Flower: not showy;
white; summer

Culture: full sun to partial shade; acid to
alkaline pH; high salt tolerance; high
drought tolerance; pest sensitive

Notes: escapes cultivation along the
beach; S. *plumieri* grows to 2' tall and is

native to Florida dunes

Uses: dune stabilization, border, mass
planting, foundation, screen, excellent
hedge

99

Schefflera arboricola (sheff-LEER-ruh ar-bor-rick-KOLE-luh)

Common name:
Dwarf Schefflera
Zone: 10a–11
Size: 8–15' tall; 6–12'
wide; moderate growth;
36 to 60" spacing
Form: round, oval;
evergreen, green foliage;
showy, orange fruit on
old plants
Flower: showy; white;
summer

Culture: full sun to full shade; tolerates
occasional wet soil; acid to slightly alkaline
pH; medium salt tolerance; high drought
tolerance; pest sensitive
Notes: makes a nice hedge; a variegated
cultivar is sometimes available; eventually
forms a fairly thick, multi-stemmed large
shrub
Uses: screen, hedge, specimen, container
or planter, border, espalier, trained as a
standard, indoors, foundation

Serenoa repens (sair-ren-NOE-uh REE-penz)

Common name:
Saw Palmetto
Zone: 8a–11; Florida
native
Size: 5–10' tall; 4–10'
wide; slow growth; 5–8'
spacing
Form: multi-stemmed
palm; evergreen, green,
silver to blue-green
foliage; yellow, black fruit

Flower: somewhat showy; white; in
warm weather
Culture: full sun to partial shade; acid to
alkaline pH; high salt tolerance; high
drought tolerance; pest resistant
Notes: the blue foliage forms are most
sought after; plants are difficult to
transplant successfully because the trunk
grows along the ground making it tough to
locate the roots
Uses: mass planting, specimen,
naturalizing, border, reclamation, accent,
barrier/screen

Spiraea cantoniensis (spy-REE-uh kan-toe-nee-EN-sis)

Common name: Reeve's Spiraea, Bridal-Wreath

Zone: 7a-9b

Size: 4-8' tall and wide; moderate growth; 5-8' spacing

Form: vase, round; deciduous, green foliage; brown fruit

Flower: very showy; white; spring

Culture: full sun; acid to slightly alkaline pH; low salt tolerance; medium drought tolerance; pest resistant

Notes: the fountain-like form makes this a nice specimen plant; allow plenty of room for growth, and plant in full sun for best flowering

Uses: border, mass planting, specimen, container or planter, foundation

Syzygium paniculatum

(sizz-ZYE-gee-um pan-nick-yoo-LAY-tum)

Common name: Brush Cherry

Zone: 10a-11

Size: 12-20' tall; 8-15' wide; moderate growth; 4-7' spacing

Form: vase, oval; evergreen, reddish new foliage turns green; edible red, black fruit

Flower: showy; white; in warm months

Culture: full sun to partial shade; acid to alkaline pH; medium salt tolerance; medium drought tolerance; pest resistant

Notes: one of the finest plants for clipping into a hedge; nice bark makes this suited for training into a multi-stemmed, small tree

Uses: bonsai, container or planter, excellent hedge, buffer or median, screen

Tabernaemontana divaricata

(tab-ber-nee-mon-TAY-nuh dye-vair-rick-KAY-tuh)

Common name: Crape Jasmine, Pinwheel Jasmine

Zone: 10b-11

Size: 6-10' tall and wide; moderate growth; 4-7' spacing

Form: round; evergreen, dark green foliage

Flower: very showy; pure white; in warm months

Culture: full sun to partial shade; acid to alkaline pH; medium salt tolerance; low drought tolerance; pest sensitive

Notes: white flowers against glossy foliage makes this a standout in the garden; variegated foliage form exists, as well as single and double flowered cultivars

Uses: border, mass planting, specimen, container or planter, hedge, foundation, trained as a standard

Tecomaria capensis (tee-koe-MAIR-ree-uh kuh-PEN-sis)

Common name: Cape Honeysuckle

Zone: 10-11

Size: variable height and spread; fast growth; 36 to 60" spacing

Form: spreading, round; evergreen, green foliage

Flower: very showy; orange, yellow, red; summer, fall

Culture: full sun; acid to alkaline pH; medium salt tolerance; medium drought tolerance; pest sensitive

Notes: grows as a viney, sprawling shrub, but can be clipped into any form

Uses: mass planting, specimen, hedge, border, container or planter, trained as a standard, espalier, attracts hummingbirds, cascade effect

Ternstroemia gymnanthera

(tern-STROE-mee-uh
jim-NANTH-er-uh)
Common name:
Cleyera, Japanese
Ternstroemia
Zone: 8-11
Size: 12-20' tall; 5-10'
wide; moderate growth;
36 to 60" spacing
Form: oval,
upright/erect; evergreen,
glossy, green foliage; showy, red fruit

Flower: somewhat showy; white; spring
Culture: sunny to mostly shaded; acid
to slightly alkaline pH; low salt tolerance;
medium drought tolerance; pest sensitive
Notes: makes an excellent hedge with its
shiny foliage and dense habit; can be
pruned into a small tree; variegated
cultivars have bright yellow and green
coloration
Uses: foundation, screen, border,
specimen, hedge

Thunbergia erecta (thun-BER-jee-uh ee-RECK-tuh)

Common name: Bush Clock Vine,
King's Mantle
Zone: 10b-11
Size: 4-6' tall; 5-8' wide; fast growth; 36 to 60"
spacing
Form: vase, round, spreading; evergreen,
green foliage
Flower: showy; purple; in warm months
Culture: full sun to partial shade; acid to
alkaline pH; medium salt tolerance; low
drought tolerance; pest resistant
Notes: usually planted and clipped into a
hedge; unclipped plants sprawl across the
ground
Uses: container or planter, superior hedge,
foundation, border, cascade effect

Tibouchina spp. (tib-boo-KYE-nuh species)

Common name:
Tibouchina,
Princess Flower
Zone: 10a-11
Size: 8-15′ tall and wide;
moderate growth;
5-10′ spacing
Form: round; evergreen,
green foliage
Flower: showy;
lavender or purple;
spring, summer, fall
Culture: full sun to partial shade; acid to
slightly alkaline pH; low salt tolerance; low
drought tolerance; pest sensitive
Notes: *T. granulosa* and *T. urvilliana* can

develop into small, dense trees; can be
grown as a perennial in north Florida;
gorgeous flowers
Uses: container or planter, border,
specimen, small flowering tree/shrub

Turnera ulmifolia (tern-NAIR-uh ul-miff-FOLE-lee-uh)

Common name:
Yellow Elder, Yellow Alder
Zone: 10-11
Size: 2-3′ tall and wide;
moderate growth; 36 to
60″ spacing
Form: round; evergreen,
green foliage
Flower: showy; yellow;
in warm months
Culture: full sun to
partial shade; acid to alkaline pH; high salt
tolerance; medium drought tolerance; pest
sensitive
Notes: can escape cultivation as seedlings
germinate readily; can be grown as a

perennial in north Florida
Uses: container or planter, foundation,
border, mass planting, groundcover, attracts
butterflies

S H R U B S

Viburnum odoratissimum

(vye-BER-num oh-duh-ruh-TISS-sim-mum)

Common name:
Sweet Viburnum

Zone: 8b-10b

Size: 15-20' tall and wide; moderate growth; 4-10' spacing

Form: round; evergreen, green foliage; red, black fruit

Flower: showy; white; summer

Culture: full sun to partial shade; acid to alkaline pH; low salt tolerance; medium drought tolerance; pest sensitive

Notes: usually grown as a hedge but is well suited for a small tree; thins in shaded locations

Uses: screen, hedge, container or planter, specimen, street tree, buffer or median

Viburnum suspensum (vye-BER-num sus-SPEN-sum)

Common name:
Sandankwa Viburnum

Zone: 8b-10b

Size: 6-10' tall and wide; moderate growth; 36 to 60" spacing

Form: upright/erect then oval to round; evergreen, green foliage; orange fruit

Flower: somewhat showy; white; winter and spring

Culture: full sun to partial shade; tolerates occasional wet soil; acid to alkaline pH; low salt tolerance; low drought tolerance; pest resistant

Notes: plants on 5' centers fill in to make a rich-looking hedge in a few years; growth often stops in the heat of the summer; does best north of zone 10

Uses: foundation, screen, border, container or planter, excellent hedge

Yucca gloriosa (YUCK-kuh glor-ree-OH-suh)

Common name: Spanish Dagger, Mound-Lily Yucca

Zone: 7-11; Florida native

Size: 6-8' tall; 4-8' wide; slow growth; 4-6' spacing

Form: upright/erect; evergreen, light green foliage

Flower: strikingly showy; white; summer

Culture: full sun to partial shade; acid to alkaline pH; high salt tolerance; high drought tolerance; pest sensitive

Notes: soft foliage bends in half creating a softer appearance than the other Yucca species; flowers are held well above the foliage for about one or two weeks each year; *Y. aloifolia* and *Y. filamentosa* are other nice natives; *Y. aloifolia* has dangerous dagger-like leaves

Uses: mass planting, specimen, naturalizing, border, accent, attracts butterflies, screen

Zamia floridana (ZAY-mee-uh flor-rid-DAY-nuh)

Common name: Coontie

Zone: 8b-11; Florida native

Size: 2-4' tall and wide; very slow growth; 36 to 60" spacing

Form: round; evergreen, green foliage; showy, brown fruit with bright red seeds

Flower: not showy

Culture: full sun to partial shade; acid to alkaline pH; high salt tolerance; high drought tolerance; pest sensitive

Notes: caterpillars of the Atala butterfly eat the foliage in south Florida, but usually with no lasting harm to the plant; foliage turns brown with temperatures in the low 20's

Uses: foundation, border, mass planting, accent, attracts butterflies, may be used indoors

TREES

Trees form the foundation for the landscape. They provide much needed shade, reduce soil erosion and water runoff, house wildlife, add a 'ceiling' to our environment and can provide food. A community with many trees builds fewer runoff retention areas because trees capture some of the rain so it never reaches the ground. Trees provide us with many other benefits.

Large shade trees such as Live Oak are best suited for a large space where there is plenty of room for root extension and canopy growth. On the other hand, small trees such as Crape Myrtle can be planted under power lines and close to patios and buildings.

When choosing large-maturing shade trees from a nursery, be sure to pick those with one dominant trunk. Trees with several trunks, each with nearly equal diameter, are far inferior and should not be planted in urban areas. They hold the potential for breaking apart in wind storms as they grow older. Several trunks are fine for small-maturing trees.

In the nursery, slip the plastic container from the root ball to check for circling roots. Do not purchase those with roots circling around the ball if those roots are larger than one-tenth the trunk diameter. Using pruning shears, cut any roots that circle the root ball. Remove the burlap or the top portion of the wire basket if trees are from a field nursery. Dig the planting hole as deep as, and about twice the width, of the root ball and backfill with native soil. No amendments are needed, only water. Water regularly for several months following planting.

Acer palmatum (AY-ser pal-MAY-tum)

Common name:
Japanese Maple
Zone: 5b-9
Size: 15-20' tall; 15-25'
wide; slow growth; 15'
spacing
Form: vase, round;
deciduous, green foliage
in summer, turning
yellow, bronze, purple, or
red in the fall; red fruit

Flower: not showy; red; spring
Culture: partial to full shade; acid to
slightly alkaline pH; low salt tolerance; low
drought tolerance; pest sensitive
Notes: hundreds of cultivars exist for size, color and shape of the canopy and foliage; autumn foliage color can be striking following cool, fall weather
Uses: specimen, planter, trained as a standard, bonsai

Acer rubrum (AY-ser ROO-brum)

Common name: Red Maple,
Swamp Maple
Zone: 4a-10b; Florida native
Size: 60-75' tall; 25-35' wide; fast growth; 25-40' spacing
Form: oval, upright/erect; deciduous, green foliage; showy, red fruit
Flower: showy; red; late winter
Culture: full sun to partial shade; tolerates wet soil; acid to neutral pH; low salt tolerance; low drought tolerance; pest sensitive
Notes: best suited for a moist spot near a source of water, but will adapt to a drier site; *A. rubrum* 'Autumn Flame' and 'October Glory' are used for their outstanding red fall color
Uses: buffer or median, screen, shade, street tree

Araucaria heterophylla

(air-ah-KAIR-ee-uh het-er-oh-FILL-uh)

Common name: Norfolk Island Pine

Zone: 10a-11

Size: 60-80' tall; 12-20' wide; fast growth; 15-20' spacing

Form: pyramidal, columnar; evergreen, green foliage; showy, green fruit is rare in Florida

Flower: not showy

Culture: full sun; acid to alkaline pH; medium salt tolerance; high drought tolerance; pest sensitive

Notes: nicely proportioned in the landscape for several years, but the tree grows too tall for many landscapes and provides no real shade; over-used in south Florida landscapes

Uses: indoors, specimen

Bauhinia blakeana (bah-HIN-ee-uh blay-kee-AY-nuh)

Common name: Hong Kong Orchid Tree

Zone: 9-11

Size: 20-30' tall; 30-40' wide; fast growth; 20-30' spacing

Form: rounded vase; evergreen, green foliage; no fruit

Flower: showy; reddish-purple; fall, winter

Culture: full sun to partial shade; acid to slightly alkaline pH; low salt tolerance; high drought tolerance; pest sensitive

Notes: other orchid trees produce fruit that makes a mess on walks and patios nearby; regular fertilizer application keeps leaves green; chlorosis develops in alkaline soil

Uses: shade, specimen, parking lot island, buffer or median

Betula nigra (BET-yoo-luh NYE-gruh)

NANCY J. BISSETT

Common name: River Birch

Zone: 4a–9a; Florida native

Size: 40–50' tall; 25–35' wide; fast growth; 25–30' spacing

Form: upright/erect, pyramidal, oval; deciduous, green foliage; brown fruit

Flower: somewhat showy; brown; spring

Culture: full sun to partial shade; tolerates wet soil; acid pH; low salt tolerance; low drought tolerance; pest resistant

Notes: can be short-lived in urban landscapes, lives longer with plenty of soil space for root expansion; grows best with plentiful soil moisture; chlorosis develops in alkaline soil

Uses: street tree, screen, shade, specimen, hedge

Bucida buceras (bew-SYE-duh bew-SER-azz)

Common name: Black Olive, Oxhorn Bucida

Zone: 10b–11

Size: 40–60' tall; 40–50' wide; moderate growth; 25–40' spacing

Form: oval, round; green foliage; black fruit

Flower: not showy; white; spring

Culture: full sun to partial shade; acid to alkaline pH; high salt tolerance; high drought tolerance; pest sensitive

Notes: over-used in urban landscapes; regular pruning (every 2–3 years) in the first 20 years is required to develop strong structure with a dominant trunk; leaves can stain cars and walks; 'Shady Lady' has smaller leaves and stays a bit smaller

Uses: street tree, shade, specimen, buffer or median, indoors

T R E E S

Bursera simaruba (ber-SER-uh sim-uh-ROO-buh)

Common name:
Gumbo Limbo
Zone: 10a-11; Florida
native
Size: 25-40' tall; 30-45'
wide; moderate growth;
25-30' spacing
Form: round; semi-
evergreen, green foliage;
red fruit
Flower: not showy;
green

Culture: full sun to partial shade; acid to alkaline pH; high salt tolerance; high drought tolerance; pest resistant
Notes: plants grown in the open are more spreading than tall with several trunks close to the ground; prune to keep branches less than about half the diameter of the trunk; bark is smooth and shiny, and peels or shreds in papery flakes
Uses: shade, specimen, street tree, parking lot island, buffer or median

Callistemon viminalis (kal-liss-STEE-mawn vim-min-NAY-liss)

Common name:
Weeping Bottlebrush
Zone: 9-11
Size: 15-20' tall and
wide; moderate growth;
15-20' spacing
Form: weeping, round;
evergreen, hairy, green
foliage; brown fruit
Flower: very showy;
red; in warm months

Culture: full sun; acid to slightly alkaline pH; medium salt tolerance; medium drought tolerance; susceptible to galls and twig blight
Notes: soft weeping habit and showy flowers make this a popular small tree for residential landscapes; watch for witches broom and twig gall which can kill the tree; will take periodic flooding; vigorous root system
Uses: hedge, specimen, screen, planter, street tree, parking lot island, buffer or median

Calophyllum brasiliense (kal-oh-FILL-um bruh-sill-ee-EN-see)

Common name: Santa Maria, Brazilian Beautyleaf
Zone: 10b-11
Size: 30-40' tall; 40-50' wide; moderate growth; 25-35' spacing
Form: oval, round, pyramidal; evergreen, green foliage; showy, green fruit
Flower: showy; white and yellow; summer
Culture: full sun to partial shade; acid to alkaline pH; high salt tolerance; medium drought tolerance; pest resistant
Notes: nicely suited for planting along streets and in the yard as a shade tree; will not dominate the yard like many of the large figs
Uses: specimen, street tree, screen, shade, hedge, espalier, parking lot island, buffer or median, planter

Carpinus caroliniana (kar-PYE-nus kair-oh-lin-ee-AY-nuh)

Common name: American Hornbeam, Blue-Beech, Ironwood
Zone: 3a-9a; Florida native
Size: 25-30' tall; 20-30' wide; slow growth; 20-25' spacing
Form: oval; deciduous green foliage; brown fruit
Flower: not showy; orange, yellow; spring
Culture: full sun to shade; tolerates occasional wet soil; acid to slightly alkaline pH; low salt tolerance; medium drought tolerance; pest resistant

Notes: nice small tree for residences or for planting under power lines along streets; bark is smooth and attractive
Uses: specimen, street tree, screen, hedge, bonsai, shade

○

Cassia fistula (KASS-ee-uh FIST-yoo-luh)

Common name: Golden-Shower
Zone: 10b-11
Size: 30-40' tall and wide; fast growth; 25-35' spacing
Form: vase, usually irregular oval, upright/erect; semi-evergreen, green foliage; long, showy, purple fruit
Flower: showy; yellow; summer
Culture: full sun; acid to alkaline pH; medium salt tolerance; medium drought tolerance; pest resistant
Notes: striking yellow flowers fill the canopy in summer; train tree to a dominant trunk by thinning competing branches; provide extra magnesium and iron on alkaline, sandy soils
Uses: street tree, shade, specimen, parking lot island

Cercis canadensis (SER-sis kan-uh-DEN-sis)

Common name: Eastern Redbud
Zone: 4b-9a; Florida native
Size: 20-30' tall; 25-35' wide; moderate growth; 20-25' spacing
Form: vase, round; deciduous, green foliage; showy, brown fruit
Flower: showy; pink, lavender or purple; early spring

Culture: full sun to partial shade; tolerates occasional wet soil; acid to alkaline pH; low salt tolerance; high drought tolerance; pest sensitive
Notes: *C. reniformis* 'Oklahoma' (deep lavender flowers) and 'Texas White' (white flowers) have shiny leaves and a nice form and are prettier than the native Redbud
Uses: street tree, planter, parking lot island, shade, specimen, buffer or median

Chionanthus virginicus (kye-oh-NANTH-us ver-JIN-ih-kuss)

Common name: Fringetree, Old-Man's-Beard

Zone: 3a-9b; Florida native

Size: 12-20' tall; 10-15' wide; slow growth; 10' spacing

Form: oval, round; deciduous, green foliage; showy, bluish-purple fruit on female trees

Flower: very showy; white; late spring

Culture: full sun to mostly shaded; tolerates occasional wet soil; acid pH; low salt tolerance; medium drought tolerance; pest sensitive

Notes: flowers best in a sunny spot; usually grown with several trunks; poisonous; *C. retusus* is a beautiful small tree with pure white flowers and showy bark

Uses: specimen, small flowering tree/large shrub

Cinnamomum camphora (sin-uh-MOE-mum kam-FOR-uh)

Common name: Camphor-Tree

Zone: 9-10b

Size: 40-50' tall; 60-90' wide; fast growth; 35-40' spacing

Form: round; evergreen, green foliage; black fruit

Flower: not showy; yellow

Culture: full sun to partial shade; acid to slightly alkaline pH; low salt tolerance; medium drought tolerance; pest sensitive

Notes: seedlings can invade native habitat; trees grow very large and can disrupt sidewalks if planted too close

Uses: screen, shade for large properties, otherwise limited due to invasive nature

Citrus spp. (SIH-trus species)

Common name:
Citrus
Zone: 9a-11
Size: 12-30' tall; 15-30'
wide; moderate growth;
15-20' spacing
Form: round; evergreen,
green foliage; showy,
orange or yellow, fruit
Flower: fragrant and
showy; white; spring

Culture: full sun; acid to slightly alkaline pH; low salt tolerance; medium drought tolerance; pest sensitive
Notes: newer selections are mostly hardy in southern part of zone 8b
Uses: hedge, screen, fruit, specimen, espalier, buffer or median, trained as a standard

Coccoloba uvifera (koe-koe-LOE-buh yoo-VIFF-er-uh)

Common name:
Sea Grape
Zone: 10b-11; Florida
native
Size: 25-40' tall and
wide; moderate growth;
20-30' spacing
Form: vase; green
foliage; showy, purple,
blue fruit on female trees
Flower: not showy;
white

Culture: full sun to partial shade; acid to alkaline pH; excellent salt tolerance; high drought tolerance; pest resistant
Notes: used regularly as a hedge along the beach; mature leaves have red veins and will turn completely red before they fall; *C. diversifolia* is also a nice native tree
Uses: street tree, specimen, shade, hedge, buffer or median, dune stabilization

Conocarpus erectus var. sericeus

(kawn-oh-KAR-pus
ee-RECK-tus variety
suh-RISS-ee-us)

Common name:
Silver Buttonwood
Zone: 10b-11; Florida
native
Size: 15-20' tall and
wide; moderate growth;
15-20' spacing
Form: vase, spreading;

evergreen, silver/gray to blue-green foliage;
showy, brownish-red fruit
Flower: not showy; white and purple
Culture: full sun; tolerates occasional
wet and brackish soil; acid to alkaline pH;
high salt tolerance; high drought tolerance;
pest resistant

Notes: the species has green foliage and
is larger than the Silver Buttonwood; both
make nice hedges and screens
Uses: specimen, street tree, screen, hedge,
parking lot island, buffer or median,
bonsai, shade, planter

Cordia sebestena (KOR-dee-uh seb-ess-TAY-nuh)

Common name:
Geiger Tree
Zone: 10b-11; Florida
native
Size: 25-30' tall; 20-25'
wide; slow growth; 20-25'
spacing
Form: round, vase;
semi-evergreen, green
foliage; showy, green fruit
Flower: very showy;
orange; summer

Culture: full sun to partial shade; acid to
alkaline pH; medium salt tolerance; high
drought tolerance; pest sensitive
Notes: geiger beetles feed on this tree

exclusively, devouring some foliage; it is
pointless to attempt control; damaged by
severe freezes, even in south Florida
Uses: planter, street tree, shade, specimen,
parking lot island, buffer or median

Cornus florida (KOR-nus FLOR-ih-duh)

Common name:
Flowering Dogwood
Zone: 5a-9a; Florida
native
Size: 20-30' tall; 25-30'
wide; moderate growth;
20' spacing
Form: round;
deciduous, green foliage;
showy, red fruit
Flower: showy; white,
pink, red; spring

Culture: mostly sunny to shade; acid to
slightly alkaline pH; low salt tolerance; low
drought tolerance; pest sensitive
Notes: powdery mildew can nearly
defoliate the tree, making it look dead by
the end of the summer; borers kill the tips
of twigs; trees in the shade grow fast but
flower less than the slower growing plants
in the sun; red and pink flowering types
grow poorly in Florida
Uses: specimen, shade

Cupaniopsis anacardiopsis

(koo-pan-nee-OP-sis
an-nuh-kar-dee-OP-sis)
Common name:
Carrotwood
Zone: 10b-11
Size: 25-35' tall and
wide; moderate growth
Form: round; evergreen,
green foliage; green,
orange fruit
Flower: not showy;
green

Culture: full sun; tolerates occasional
wet soil; acid to slightly alkaline pH;
medium salt tolerance; medium drought
tolerance; pest resistant
Notes: well adapted to Florida's climate;
this plant invades native habitat; fruit
makes a mess on pavement and walks
Uses: not recommended due to invasive
nature; many communities enacted
ordinances prohibiting planting this tree

x *Cupressocyparis leylandii*

(koo-press-so-SIP-air-iss lay-LAN-dee-eye)
Common name: Leyland Cypress
Zone: 6a-10a
Size: 35-50' tall; 15-25' wide; fast growth; 10-15' spacing
Form: oval, columnar; evergreen, green foliage; brown cone
Flower: not showy
Culture: full sun to partial shade; acid to alkaline pH; medium salt tolerance; medium drought tolerance; pest sensitive
Notes: foliage occasionally dies back from a twig blight; does best in full sun; *J. silicicola* is a native plant that looks similar to Leyland Cypress
Uses: specimen, screen, hedge, buffer or median

Cupressus sempervirens (koo-PRESS-us sem-per-VYE-renz)

Common name: Italian Cypress
Zone: 7b-10b
Size: 40-60' tall; 3-6' wide; moderate growth; 4-5' spacing
Form: columnar; evergreen, green foliage
Flower: not showy
Culture: full sun; acid to alkaline pH; medium salt tolerance; medium drought tolerance; pest sensitive
Notes: watch for mite infestation, especially in hot weather; does best north of zone 10b
Uses: screen, accent

T R E E S ⬤

Delonix regia (dee-LOE-nicks REE-jee-uh)

Common name:
Royal Poinciana
Zone: 10b-11
Size: 35-40' tall; 40-60'
wide; fast growth; 30-45'
spacing
Form: vase, spreading;
semi-evergreen, green
foliage; showy, brown
fruit
Flower: very showy;
red and orange; early summer

Culture: full sun; acid to alkaline pH;
medium salt tolerance; high drought
tolerance; pest resistant
Notes: prune every 2-3 years for about
20 years to develop strong structure; thin
the branches that develop; keep branches
less than about half the trunk diameter
using thinning cuts; roots suppress turf
growth
Uses: street tree, specimen, shade

Eriobotrya japonica (air-ee-oh-BOT-ree-uh juh-PAWN-ih-kuh)

Common name:
Loquat
Zone: 8a-11
Size: 20-30' tall; 30-35'
wide; moderate growth;
25' spacing
Form: round; evergreen,
green foliage; showy,
yellow to orange edible
fruit
Flower: showy; creamy
white; fall and winter

Culture: full sun to partial shade; acid to
alkaline pH; medium salt tolerance; high
drought tolerance; pest and disease
sensitive
Notes: fire blight kills twigs throughout
the canopy, especially if air circulation is
poor and foliage is kept wet; mushroom
root rot kills trees in 5-10 days
Uses: trained as a standard, street tree,
screen, fruit, specimen, espalier, planter,
buffer or median

Ficus benjamina (FYE-kuss ben-juh-MYE-nuh)

Common name:
Weeping Fig
Zone: 10b-11
Size: 45-60' tall; 60-100' wide; fast growth
Form: weeping, round, spreading; green foliage; red fruit
Flower: not showy
Culture: full sun to shade; tolerates occasional

wet soil; acid to alkaline pH; medium salt tolerance; high drought tolerance; pest resistant
Notes: due to its large, aggressive habit, it is best suited for landscapes with plenty of room; *F. retusa* is slightly more cold tolerant; both have invasive roots and seeds are capable of germinating in the landscape; roots are less invasive when used as a hedge
Uses: street tree, shade tree, planter, hedge, indoors, bonsai

Ficus elastica (FYE-kuss ee-LASS-tick-uh)

Common name:
Rubber-Tree,
India-Rubber Fig
Zone: 10b-11
Size: 30-45' tall and wide; fast growth; 30-40' spacing
Form: oval; evergreen, green foliage; green fruit
Flower: not showy
Culture: full sun to

partial shade; tolerates occasional wet soil; acid to alkaline pH; medium salt tolerance; high drought tolerance; pest resistant
Notes: moderately large tree suited for a landscape with plenty of room; does not grow quite as fast as some of the other Figs; variegated cultivars have brightly colored yellow and green foliage
Uses: shade, trained as a standard, indoors, screen, specimen, container or planter, espalier, buffer or median

Ficus lyrata (FYE-kuss lye-RAY-tuh)

Common name:
Fiddleleaf Fig
Zone: 10b-11
Size: 25-40' tall and
wide; moderate growth;
30-40' spacing
Form: vase, round,
spreading; green foliage;
green fruit
Flower: not showy
Culture: full sun to

partial shade; tolerates occasional wet soil;
acid to alkaline pH; medium salt tolerance;
high drought tolerance; pest resistant
Notes: common as a house plant but
also makes a dense shade tree; prune so
branches are spaced along a dominant,
central trunk
Uses: indoors, deck or patio, specimen,
container or planter, espalier, buffer or
median, street tree, shade

Ficus retusa (microcarpa) (FYE-kuss ree-TOO-suh)

Common name:
Cuban Laurel, Indian
Laurel
Zone: 10a-11
Size: 50-60' tall; 60-100'
wide; fast growth
Form: round, vase,
spreading; green foliage;
red fruit
Flower: not showy
Culture: full sun to

partial shade; tolerates occasional wet soil;
acid to alkaline pH; medium salt tolerance;
high drought tolerance; pest sensitive
Notes: due to its large, aggressive habit, it
is best suited for landscapes with plenty of
room; aerial roots invade the landscape;
seeds germinate in the landscape and can
become invasive
Uses: shade, hedge, topiary, container,
indoors

Fraxinus pennsylvanica (FRACK-sih-nus pen-sill-VAN-ih-kuh)

Common name: Green Ash
Zone: 3a-9a; Florida native
Size: 60-70' tall; 45-50' wide; fast growth; 35-40' spacing
Form: upright/erect, oval; deciduous, green foliage; showy, tan fruit
Flower: not showy; green
Culture: full sun; tolerates wet soil; acid to alkaline pH; medium salt tolerance; medium drought tolerance; pest sensitive
Notes: the related *F. americana* can become a huge tree with a 6' diameter trunk in north Florida; both plants have showy fall color in most years
Uses: shade, street tree, parking lot island, buffer or median

Ilex x attenuata 'East Palatka'

(EYE-lecks x uh-ten-yoo-AY-tuh)
Common name: 'East Palatka' Holly
Zone: 7-10; Florida native
Size: 30-45' tall; 10-15' wide; moderate growth; 10-15' spacing
Form: pyramidal, columnar; evergreen, green foliage; showy, red fruit on female plants
Flower: not showy; white; spring
Culture: full sun to partial shade; acid pH; medium salt tolerance; medium drought tolerance; pest sensitive
Notes: a serious witches broom, induced by a fungus which kills trees, has devastated many plants in parts of southwest Florida; 'Savannah' Holly is similar, popular and sensitive to the fungus
Uses: planter, screen, specimen, street tree, parking lot island, buffer or median

Jacaranda mimosifolia

(jack-uh-RAN-duh mih-moe-sih-FOLE-ee-uh)

Common name:
Jacaranda

Zone: 9b-11

Size: 25-40' tall; 45-60' wide; fast growth; 25-40' spacing

Form: vase, spreading; deciduous, green foliage; brown fruit

Flower: showy; lavender to purple; summer

Culture: full sun; acid to slightly alkaline pH; low salt tolerance; high drought tolerance; disease sensitive

Notes: thin branches from limbs that compete with the dominant trunk; decomposing flowers can make a slippery mess on a sidewalk under the tree, but fallen flowers are beautiful when displayed on a lawn

Uses: parking lot island, street tree, shade, specimen

Juniperus silicicola (joo-NIP-er-us sill-liss-sih-KOLE-uh)

Common name: Southern Red Cedar

Zone: 8a-10b; Florida native

Size: 30-40' tall; 20-30' wide; moderate growth; 10-20' spacing

Form: variable, pyramidal, columnar, oval; evergreen, green foliage; showy, purplish-blue fruit

Flower: not showy

Culture: full sun to partial shade; acid to alkaline pH; high salt tolerance; high drought tolerance; pest sensitive

Notes: birds quickly devour fruit; plant form varies greatly from one tree to the next; may be more disease resistant than Leyland Cypress

Uses: screen, street tree, buffer or median

Koelreuteria elegans (kole-roo-TEER-ee-uh ELL-eh-ganz)

Common name:
Golden Rain Tree
Zone: 9b-11
Size: 25-40' tall; 35-50' wide; fast growth; 20-30' spacing
Form: round; deciduous, green foliage; showy, pink fruit for two weeks in fall
Flower: very showy; yellow; summer

Culture: full sun; tolerates occasional wet soil; acid to alkaline pH; low salt tolerance; medium drought tolerance; pest sensitive
Notes: thousands of seedlings germinate everywhere near the tree; *K. paniculata* and *K. bipinnata* are best suited for north Florida and are just as beautiful in flower
Uses: parking lot island, shade, specimen, street tree, buffer or median

Lagerstroemia indica **hybrids**

(lay-ger-STREE-mee-uh IN-dih-kuh)
Common name: Crape Myrtle
Zone: 7a-10b
Size: 10-30' tall; 15-30' wide; moderate growth; 15-20' spacing
Form: vase; deciduous, green foliage; showy, brown fruit
Flower: showy; white, pink, purple, lavender or red; summer
Culture: full sun; acid to alkaline pH; low salt tolerance; high drought tolerance; pest sensitive
Notes: 'Natchez', Muskogee' and 'Tuskegee' resist mildew, and are the best cultivars for zone 10; 'Fantasy' and 'Townhouse' are superior cultivars, but are largely untested in zones 9 and 10

Litchi chinensis (LEE-chee chih-NEN-sis)

Common name:
Lychee
Zone: 10a-11
Size: 25-40' tall and
wide; slow growth; 20-30'
spacing
Form: round, spreading;
evergreen, green foliage;
showy, delicious, red fruit
Flower: not showy;
white; spring

Culture: full sun; tolerates occasional
wet soil; acid to slightly alkaline pH; low
salt tolerance; medium drought tolerance;
pest sensitive

Notes: prized for its wonderfully
succulent fruit; beautiful shade tree
Uses: fruit, specimen, shade, screen,
planter

Lysiloma latisiliqua (lye-sih-LOE-muh lat-tis-suh-LEE-kwa)

Common name:
Wild Tamarind, Bahama
Lysiloma
Zone: 10b-11; Florida
native
Size: 40-60' tall; 30-45'
wide; fast growth; 25-30'
spacing
Form: vase, weeping;
evergreen, green foliage;
showy, brown fruit

Flower: not showy; fragrant; white
Culture: full sun to partial shade; acid to
alkaline pH; high salt tolerance; high
drought tolerance; pest resistant
Notes: outstanding weeping habit; prune

so limbs remain less than half the trunk
diameter and space major branches along
the trunk
Uses: street tree, shade, buffer or median,
specimen, parking lot island

Magnolia grandiflora (mag-NO-lee-uh gran-dih-FLOR-uh)

Common name: Southern Magnolia

Zone: 7a-10b; Florida native

Size: 40-80' tall; 15-40' wide; moderate growth; 25-40' spacing

Form: pyramidal, oval; evergreen, green foliage; showy, brown, red fruit

Flower: showy and slightly fragrant; white; summer

Culture: full sun to partial shade; tolerates occasional wet soil; acid to slightly alkaline pH; high salt tolerance; medium drought tolerance; pest sensitive

Notes: some cultivars have narrow canopies like 'Hasse' and 'Mgtig', others have brown undersides like 'Bracken's Brown Beauty' and 'D.D. Blanchard'

Uses: shade, specimen, street tree, screen, buffer or median

Magnolia x soulangiana

(mag-NO-lee-uh x soo-lan-jee-AY-nuh)

Common name: Saucer Magnolia

Zone: 5a-9a

Size: 20-25' tall; 15-25' wide; moderate growth; 10-15' spacing

Form: upright/erect, round; deciduous, green foliage; red fruit

Flower: showy; pink, lavender or purple, white; late winter

Culture: full sun to partial shade; acid pH; low salt tolerance; low drought tolerance; disease sensitive

Notes: the spectacular flowers in February are always welcome, however, they are sometimes killed by late freezes or frosts

Uses: specimen, planter, espalier

Podocarpus macrophyllus

(poe-doe-KAR-pus mack-roe-FILL-us)

Common name: Podocarpus, Japanese Yew

Zone: 7-11

Size: 30-40' tall; 20-25' wide; moderate growth; 20-25' spacing

Form: round; evergreen, green foliage; edible, purple fruit

Flower: not showy; creamy yellow

Culture: full sun to mostly shaded; acid to alkaline pH; medium salt tolerance; medium drought tolerance; pest sensitive

Notes: mostly grown as a shrub, but it also makes a nice, small tree for difficult sites, such as along streets and in parking lot islands

Uses: buffer or median, screen, street tree, specimen, shade, hedge, espalier, parking lot island, trained as a standard

Pongamia pinnata (pawn-GAM-ee-uh pih-NAY-tuh)

Common name: Pongam, Karum Tree, Poonga-Oil Tree

Zone: 10b-11

Size: 35-40' tall and wide; fast growth; 30-35' spacing

Form: round, spreading; evergreen, green foliage; showy, brown fruit

Flower: showy; pink, lavender, white; spring

Culture: full sun; acid to slightly alkaline pH; medium salt tolerance; high drought tolerance; pest sensitive

Notes: popular tree due to fast growth; be sure to prune regularly to keep branches smaller than half the diameter of the trunk; storms wreck trees not properly pruned

Uses: specimen, shade, buffer or median

Psidium littorale (SID-ee-um lit-aw-RAY-lee)

Common name:
Cattley Guava, Strawberry Guava

Zone: 10a–11

Size: 15-25' tall; 12-20' wide; moderate growth; 20-25' spacing

Form: round, vase; evergreen, green foliage; showy, red fruit

Flower: somewhat showy; white; spring

Culture: full sun to partial shade; tolerates occasional wet soil; acid to alkaline pH; low salt tolerance; high drought tolerance; pest sensitive

Notes: showy, smooth bark makes this plant well adapted for use as a small tree; fruit is edible and tasty; trees can escape cultivation

Uses: shade, specimen, espalier, fruit, container or planter, buffer or median

Pyrus calleryana **'Bradford'** (PIE-rus kal-ler-ee-AY-nuh)

Common name: 'Bradford' Callery Pear

Zone: 5a-9a

Size: 30-40' tall and wide; fast growth; 25-30' spacing

Form: oval, round; deciduous, green foliage; tan, brown fruit

Flower: showy; white; spring

Culture: full sun; tolerates occasional wet soil; acid to alkaline pH; low salt tolerance; medium drought tolerance; pest resistant

Notes: trees often fall apart as they reach 25-30 years old; other cultivars are less inclined to self-destruct, but are generally more sensitive to fireblight disease; best for north Florida where fall color can be spectacular

Uses: street tree, screen, shade, specimen, parking lot island, buffer or median

Quercus laurifolia (KWERK-us lar-ih-FOLE-ee-uh)

Common name:
Laurel Oak
Zone: 6b-10a; Florida native
Size: 60-70' tall; 40-60' wide; fast growth; 30-40' spacing
Form: round, oval; semi-evergreen, green foliage; brown fruit
Flower: not showy; green; spring

Culture: full sun to partial shade; tolerates occasional wet soil; acid to slightly alkaline pH; low salt tolerance; high drought tolerance; pest resistant
Notes: *Q. hemisphaerica* is very similar but does not tolerate poor drainage well; both have a relatively short life of about 60 years in urban landscapes
Uses: shade, parking lot island, buffer or median, street tree

Quercus shumardii (KWERK-us shoo-MAR-dee-eye)

Common name: Shumard Oak
Zone: 5b-9a; Florida native
Size: 55-80' tall; 40-50' wide; fast growth; 25-35' spacing
Form: round, oval; deciduous, green foliage
Flower: not showy; green; spring
Culture: full sun; tolerates occasional wet soil; acid to alkaline pH; low salt tolerance; high drought tolerance; pest sensitive
Notes: bright red fall color in north Florida; generally performs poorly in central Florida; prune to one dominant trunk by thinning or drop-crotching stems that grow parallel with the trunk
Uses: street tree, shade, specimen, parking lot island, buffer or median

Quercus virginiana (KWERK-us ver-jin-ee-AY-nuh)

Common name: Southern Live Oak, Live Oak

Zone: 7b-11; Florida native

Size: 40-80' tall; 60-120' wide; moderate growth; 30-45' spacing

Form: spreading, round; semi-evergreen, green foliage; brown fruit

Flower: not showy; green; spring

Culture: full sun to partial shade; tolerates occasional wet soil; acid to alkaline pH; high salt tolerance; high drought tolerance; pest sensitive

Notes: to develop a strong structure, prune regularly (every 2-3 years) for the first 20 years; thin any branches that grow larger than about half the size of the trunk

Uses: street tree, shade, specimen, parking lot island, buffer or median

Ravenala madagascariensis

(rav-eh-NAY-luh mad-uh-gas-kar-ee-EN-sis)

Common name: Traveler's Tree

Zone: 10b-11

Size: 15-25' tall; 15-18' wide; moderate growth; 15' spacing

Form: palm-like; evergreen, green foliage

Flower: showy; white; spring, summer, fall

Culture: full sun to partial shade; acid to slightly alkaline pH; low salt tolerance; medium drought tolerance; pest sensitive

Notes: large foliage tears in the wind but causes no real harm to the plant; plant in a protected area to keep leaves from tearing; damaged by hard freezes

Uses: specimen, container or planter

T R E E S

Schefflera actinophylla (shef-LEER-uh ack-tin-oh-FILL-uh)

Common name: Schefflera, Queensland
Umbrella Tree

Zone: 10a-11

Size: 30-40' tall; 10-15' wide; fast growth

Form: upright/erect; evergreen, green foliage;
showy, purple, red fruit

Flower: showy; red; summer

Culture: full sun to partial shade; tolerates
occasional wet soil; acid to slightly alkaline pH;
medium salt tolerance; high drought tolerance;
pest sensitive

Notes: seeds germinate readily in nearby
landscapes and become weeds; the plant has
invaded ditch banks and woodlands in south
Florida and has the potential to spread rapidly

Uses: indoors, large shrub, small tree

Strelitzia nicolai (streh-LIT-see-uh NICK-oh-lye)

Common name: White Bird of Paradise,
Giant Bird of Paradise

Zone: 10a-11

Size: 20-30' tall; 6-10' wide; moderate growth;
10-15' spacing

Form: upright/erect, palm-like; evergreen,
green foliage

Flower: showy; white; summer, fall

Culture: full sun to partial shade; acid to
slightly alkaline pH; medium salt tolerance;
high drought tolerance; pest sensitive

Notes: foliage tears in the wind; provide
plenty of moisture; white flowers are produced
among the foliage; can be used in zone 9b with
protection

Uses: specimen, container or planter, indoors

135

Swietenia mahagoni (swee-TEEN-ee-uh mah-HAH-go-nye)

Common name: Mahogany, West Indies Mahogany

Zone: 10b-11; Florida native

Size: 40-50' tall; 40-60' wide; fast growth; 30-40' spacing

Form: round; evergreen, green foliage; showy, brown fruit

Flower: not showy; green-yellow; spring

Culture: full sun to partial shade; tolerates occasional wet soil; acid to alkaline pH; high salt tolerance; high drought tolerance; pest sensitive

Notes: insects often damage the branch tips, causing an undesirable proliferation of branches; webworms damage the foliage

Uses: street tree, screen, shade, parking lot island, buffer or median

Tabebuia caraiba (tab-eh-BOO-yuh kuh-RYE-buh)

Common name: Silver Trumpet Tree, Yellow Tab

Zone: 10a-11

Size: 15-25' tall; 10-20' wide; moderate growth; 15-20' spacing

Form: oval, often irregular; semi-evergreen, gray-green foliage; brown fruit

Flower: exceptionally showy; yellow; spring

Culture: full sun to partial shade; acid to alkaline pH; medium salt tolerance; high drought tolerance; pest resistant

Notes: one of the most glorious flowering trees for south Florida landscapes; leaves drop just before flowers emerge

Uses: street tree, specimen, parking lot island, buffer or median, container or planter

T R E E S

Tabebuia heterophylla (tab-eh-BOO-yuh he-teh-roh-FYE-la)

Common name: Pink Trumpet Tree
Zone: 10a-11
Size: 20-30' tall; 20-25' wide; moderate growth; 15-20' spacing
Form: oval; evergreen, green foliage; showy, green, white/gray fruit
Flower: showy; pink, white; spring, summer
Culture: full sun; acid to alkaline pH; medium salt tolerance; high drought tolerance; pest resistant
Notes: this is one of the more popular, but least hardy, Trumpet trees due to the delicate pink flower; the rounded canopy makes this a nice tree for a formal landscape
Uses: specimen, street tree, parking lot island, buffer or median

Tabebuia impetiginosa

(tab-eh-BOO-yuh im-pet-ih-jih-NO-suh)
Common name: Purple Tabebuia, Ipe
Zone: 10a-11
Size: 12-18' tall; 10-15' wide; slow growth; 15-20' spacing
Form: round; semi-evergreen, green foliage

Flower: very showy; pinkish-purple; spring
Culture: full sun; acid to slightly alkaline pH; medium salt tolerance; high drought tolerance; pest resistant

Notes: spectacular in flower; open growth habit
Uses: specimen, street tree, buffer or median, parking lot island, container or planter

Taxodium ascendens (tack-SO-dee-um uh-SEN-denz)

Common name: Pond Cypress

Zone: 5b-10b; Florida native

Size: 50-60' tall; 10-15' wide; moderate growth; 15-20' spacing

Form: pyramidal, upright/erect, columnar; deciduous, green foliage

Flower: not showy

Culture: full sun to partial shade; tolerates flooding; acid to slightly alkaline pH; medium salt tolerance; high drought tolerance; pest resistant

Notes: this tree is becoming more

popular as people discover its versatility; the tree adapts to wet or dry sites; fall color is usually yellow-brown and showy in most years

Uses: street tree, specimen, retention pond

Taxodium distichum (tack-SO-dee-um DISS-tick-um)

Common name: Bald Cypress

Zone: 5a-10b; Florida native

Size: 60-80' tall; 25-35' wide; moderate growth; 15-25' spacing

Form: pyramidal, upright/erect; deciduous, green foliage; brown, green fruit

Flower: not showy; brown

Culture: full sun; tolerates flooding; acid to slightly alkaline pH; medium salt tolerance; high drought tolerance; pest resistant

Notes: adapts to wet or dry sites; showy yellow-brown fall color; trees grow slowly in water but they survive; surprisingly tolerant of shearing

Uses: street tree, retention pond, screen, specimen, parking lot island, buffer or median, shade, hedge

T R E E S

Ulmus parvifolia (UL-mus par-vih-FOLE-ee-uh)

Common name: Chinese Elm, Lacebark Elm

Zone: 5b-10b

Size: 40-50' tall and wide; moderate growth; 25-40' spacing

Form: variable, vase, round; evergreen (south Florida) deciduous (north), green foliage; brown fruit

Flower: not showy; green; summer

Culture: full sun to partial shade; tolerates occasional wet soil; acid to alkaline pH; low salt tolerance; high drought tolerance; pest sensitive

Notes: bark on some trees is showy; 'Athena' is round to about 30' tall; 'Allee' is 70' tall and upright and well suited for streets; since 'Drake' is weeping, it is poorly suited for planting close to parking lots and streets; many other cultivars exist

Uses: street tree, shade, specimen, parking lot island, buffer or median, bonsai

Yucca elephantipes (YUCK-uh ell-uh-fan-TYE-peez)

Common name: Spineless Yucca, Soft-Tip Yucca

Zone: 9b-11

Size: 20-30' tall; 10-15' wide; moderate growth; 15-20' spacing

Form: upright/erect; evergreen, green foliage

Flower: very showy; white; summer, fall

Culture: full sun to partial shade; acid to alkaline pH; medium salt tolerance; high drought tolerance; pest sensitive

Notes: foliage does not have the sharp tips as other Yuccas do; eventually grows to a large size; 'Variegata' has variegated foliage

Uses: indoors, specimen, accent, container or planter, buffer or median

VINES

Of the many vines capable of growing in Florida, several stand out because of their beautiful flowers. Many vines grow extremely fast and can become a nuisance if they are not placed properly. For example, the Passion Flower vine can grow 20 to 30 feet in one year, covering everything in its path. Place vines in a spot that will be easy to access so you can trim them regularly to keep them in bounds. It is best to keep vines away from shrubs to prevent them from tangling with the foliage. Most vines climb up tree trunks, arbors and fences where they display their flowers beautifully. Flowers and new growth tend to accumulate at the top of the fence or arbor leaving the lower portions with sparse growth.

Allamanda cathartica (al-luh-MAN-duh kath-AR-tick-kuh)

Common name:
Yellow Allamanda

Zone: 10a-11

Size: grows on trellis to any height; fast growth; 36 to 60" spacing

Form: spreading; evergreen, green foliage; green fruit

Flower: very showy; yellow; nearly year-round

Culture: full sun; acid to alkaline pH; low salt tolerance; medium drought tolerance; pest sensitive

Notes: quickly covers a fence or arbor with yellow flowers nearly all year; very poisonous

Uses: container or planter, ground cover, cascade effect, hanging basket

Mandevilla splendens (man-dah-VILL-ah SPLEN-denz)

Common name:
Mandevilla, Pink Allamanda

Zone: 10a-11

Size: grows on trellis to any height; fast growth; 36 to 60" spacing

Form: spreading; evergreen, green foliage; green fruit

Flower: very showy; pink or red; nearly year-round

Culture: full sun; acid to alkaline pH; medium salt tolerance; high drought tolerance; pest sensitive

Notes: quickly covers a fence or arbor with flowers nearly all year

Uses: container or planter, ground cover, cascade effect, hanging basket

O V I N E S

Passiflora coccinea (pass-siff-FLOR-ruh kock-SIN-nee-uh)

Common name:
Red Passion Flower,
Passion Vine
Zone: 10a-11
Size: grows on trellis to
any height; rapid growth;
more than 60" spacing
Form: spreading; semi-
evergreen, green foliage;
showy, yellow fruit
Flower: very showy; red;
summer, fall

Culture: full sun; tolerates occasional wet soil; acid to slightly alkaline pH; low salt tolerance; medium drought tolerance; pest sensitive
Notes: caterpillars eat foliage and become beautiful butterflies; may not flower reliably in some areas; can grow 20-30 feet in one year
Uses: screen, attracts butterflies and hummingbirds, cascade effect

Pyrostegia venusta (pye-roe-STEEG-ee-uh ven-NUSS-tuh)

Common name:
Flame Vine
Zone: 10-11
Size: 80' tall or more; fast
growth; more than 60"
spacing
Form: spreading;
evergreen, green foliage
Flower: showy; orange;
winter, spring
Culture: full sun to

partial shade; acid to alkaline pH; low salt tolerance; high drought tolerance; pest resistant
Notes: fast growth and bright flowers make this a popular plant to cover fences and arbors; prune severely after flowering
Uses: espalier, on arbors and fences

Thunbergia grandiflora (thun-BER-jee-uh gran-diff-FLOR-ruh)

Common name:
Bengal Clock Vine,
Sky Vine
Zone: 10-11
Size: 40' or taller; fast
growth; more than 60"
spacing
Form: spreading;
evergreen, green foliage
Flower: showy; bluish-
purple; nearly year-round

Culture: full sun to partial shade; acid to alkaline pH; low salt tolerance; medium drought tolerance; pest resistant
Notes: can grow 15-20' in one year; can quickly become a weed but has beautiful flowers; quickly covers a fence or a nearby tree
Uses: espalier, cascade effect, container or planter

Trachelospermum jasminoides

(tray-kell-loe-SPER-mum jaz-min-NOY-deez)

Common name: Confederate Jasmine,
Star Jasmine
Zone: 8-10b
Size: 80' tall or more; fast growth; more than 60" spacing
Form: spreading; evergreen, green or variegated foliage
Flower: showy and fragrant; white; spring
Culture: full sun to partial shade; acid to alkaline pH; medium salt tolerance; medium drought tolerance; pest resistant
Notes: quickly covers an arbor or climbs up a tree trunk; can grow into and cover nearby shrubs and trees
Uses: covers an arbor; cascade effect; attracts bees

FOLIAGE

Plants are commonly used indoors in homes, offices and malls because their foliage is highly decorative and they tolerate relatively low light conditions, at least for a period of time. Despite this tolerance to shade, most plants perform best in a bright spot indoors. Many can also be placed in the garden in a protected location. Foliage can be torn on large-leaved plants, such as Dieffenbachia, in a windy, open location. Plants such as the Ponytail, some Bromeliads and some Dracaenas can be grown in full sun in a relatively open location because their foliage is tougher.

Foliage plants are easy to grow indoors and can last several years, provided they are not over-watered. Although pests such as mites and mealy-bugs occasionally infest leaves and stems, it is frequent watering that usually leads to their demise. Let the container media dry out slightly before watering. It is better to wait until you see plants wilt slightly than to water when you 'think' they need water.

Many other plants presented in other sections of this book can be used indoors as well. Consult Appendix 6, p. 158, for a list of these plants.

Aglaonema commutatum

(ag-lay-oh-NEE-muh
komm-mew-TAY-tum)

Common name:
Aglaonema

Zone: 10b-11

Size: 2-3′ tall and wide;
moderate growth; 24 to 36″
spacing

Form: upright/erect;
variegated, green,
silver/gray foliage; showy,
red fruit

Flower: not showy; green, white

Culture: full shade outdoors, sunny spot
indoors; low salt tolerance; low drought
tolerance; pest sensitive

Notes: does well in homes, offices and
malls; numerous Aglaonemas are available
with different foliage colorations, most with
similar cultural requirements

Uses: foundation, border, mass planting,
container, groundcover, edging, indoors

Alocasia spp. (al-loe-KAY-zhee-uh species)

Common name:
Elephant's Ear

Zone: 10b-11

Size: 2-10′ tall; 1-10′
wide; fast growth; 36 to 60″
spacing

Form: upright/erect;
green or variegated foliage

Flower: showy; green,
white, purple

Culture: full sun to

shade; some types tolerate wet soil; low salt
tolerance; low drought tolerance; pest
resistant

Notes: place in a sunny spot indoors; a
variety of foliage colors and plant sizes are
available; foliage on some types is 3-6′ long

Uses: specimen, border, container, accent,
indoors

Anthurium andraeanum (an-THUR-ree-um an-dree-AY-num)

Common name:
Tailflower, Flamingo Flower
Zone: 10b-11
Size: 2-3' tall and wide;
slow growth; 18 to 24"
spacing
Form: upright/erect;
green foliage; red fruit
Flower: showy; red,
pink, white or salmon
Culture: partial to full

shade; acid to neutral pH; low salt tolerance; medium drought tolerance; pest sensitive
Notes: makes a wonderful house plant in a bright, humid spot

Uses: mass planting, specimen, container or planter, border, groundcover, cut flowers, accent, edging, indoors

Beaucarnea recurvata (boe-KAR-nee-uh reck-kurr-VAY-tuh)

Common name:
Ponytail
Zone: 9-11
Size: 12-25' tall; 10-15'
wide; slow growth; 8-10'
spacing
Form: palm-like,
upright/erect; green foliage
Flower: showy; creamy-
white
Culture: full sun to

partial shade; acid to alkaline pH; medium salt tolerance; high drought tolerance; pest resistant
Notes: makes a great accent in the garden;

place in a sunny spot indoors; often, erroneously called a palm
Uses: specimen, container or planter; indoors

F O L I A G E

Cordyline terminalis (kor-dill-LYE-nee ter-min-NAY-liss)

Common name:
Ti Plant
Zone: 10b-11
Size: 3-10' tall; 2-4' wide;
moderate growth; 36 to 60"
spacing
Form: upright/erect;
striped, purple/red or
green, striped foliage; red
fruit
Flower: not showy;
yellow, white, pink; fall
Culture: full sun to partial shade; acid to
slightly alkaline pH; low salt tolerance;
medium drought tolerance; pest sensitive
Notes: plants are grown for their brightly
colored foliage; mass several together in the
garden or place in a pot for indoor use
Uses: border, specimen, container, indoors,
accent, mass planting

Dieffenbachia spp. (deef-fen-BACK-kee-uh species)

Common name: Dumbcane
Zone: 10b-11
Size: 4-8' tall; 2-3' wide; moderate growth; 24 to
36" spacing
Form: upright/erect; variegated, green foliage;
red fruit
Flower: not showy; green
Culture: partial to full shade; acid to neutral
pH; low salt tolerance; low drought tolerance;
pest sensitive
Notes: showy foliage and good shade tolerance
make this popular indoors; can also be placed in
a protected spot in the garden; many cultivars are
available with various foliage coloration patterns
Uses: border, specimen, mass planting, container,
accent, indoors

Dracaena deremensis (druh-SEEN-nuh dair-rem-MEN-sis)

Common name: Dracaena
Zone: 10b-11
Size: 8-12′ tall; 2-5′ wide; moderate growth; 24 to 36″ spacing
Form: upright/erect; green or striped foliage; red fruit
Flower: not showy; yellow, white
Culture: partial to full shade; tolerates occasional wet soil; acid to slightly alkaline pH; low salt tolerance; medium drought tolerance; pest resistant
Notes: wonderful accent for indoors in a bright spot
Uses: mass planting, specimen, container, border, indoors

Dracaena fragrans 'Massangeana'

(druh-SEEN-nuh FRAY-grunz)

Common name: Corn Plant, Fragrant Dracaena
Zone: 10b-11
Size: 5-15′ tall; 2-3′ wide; slow growth; 18 to 24″ spacing
Form: upright/erect; green foliage usually with a wide stripe
Flower: showy and very fragrant; yellow, creamy-white
Culture: partial to full shade; acid to slightly alkaline pH; low salt tolerance; medium drought tolerance; pest resistant
Notes: grows for many years as a house plant
Uses: screen, mass planting, specimen, container, indoors, accent

Dracaena reflexa (druh-SEEN-nuh ree-FLECK-suh)

Common name: Reflexed Dracaena
Zone: 10b-11
Size: 8-15' tall; 6-10' wide; slow growth; space more than 60" apart
Form: upright/erect, oval; green or variegated foliage
Flower: not showy; white
Culture: full sun to partial shade; acid to alkaline pH; low salt tolerance; high drought tolerance; pest resistant
Notes: grows as a tree outdoors in south Florida
Uses: container, specimen, border, accent, indoors, cut foliage

Epipremnum aureum (epp-pip-PREM-num AR-ree-um)

Common name: Golden Pothos, Pothos
Zone: 10a-11
Size: 6" as a groundcover; fast growth; 24 to 36" spacing
Form: prostrate (flat) or spreading groundcover or vine; green and yellow, variegated foliage
Flower: not showy; creamy white, green
Culture: partial to full shade; tolerates occasional wet soil; acid to slightly alkaline pH; medium salt tolerance; high drought tolerance; pest resistant
Notes: grows as a groundcover but will climb into shrubs and trees; stem becomes several inches thick and leaves 12" long when climbing on tree trunks
Uses: mass planting, groundcover, container, naturalizing, indoors, cut foliage, hanging basket

Guzmania lingulata (guz-MAHN-ee-a ling-gew-LAH-ta)

Common name: Orange Star

Zone: 10-11

Size: 12-18" tall and wide; slow growth; 12-18" spacing

Form: vase; yellow-green foliage

Flower: showy; orange-red, purple-red

Culture: partial to full shade; acid to alkaline pH; low salt tolerance; low drought tolerance; pest resistant

Notes: has brilliant colored bracts; Guzmania is one of many popular Bromeliads

Uses: specimen, container, groundcover, mass planting, border, indoors, accent

Maranta leuconeura (muh-RAN-tuh loo-koe-NOOR-ruh)

Common name: Prayer Plant, Rabbit Tracks

Zone: 10b-11

Size: 6"-2' tall; 2-4' wide; slow to medium growth; 24 to 36" spacing

Form: spreading; green, variegated foliage; brown fruit

Flower: not showy; white and purple

Culture: partial to full shade; acid pH; low salt tolerance; low drought tolerance; pest sensitive

Notes: watch for mite infestations; may die back in winter, but resprout in spring

Uses: groundcover, container, mass planting, edging, hanging basket, indoors, cascade effect

F O L I A G E

Neoregelia spectabilis

(nee-oh-redge-JEEL-lee-uh
speck-TAB-bill-liss)

Common name:
Painted Fingernail Plant
Zone: 10a-11
Size: 12-18" tall; 2' wide;
slow growth; 18 to 24"
spacing
Form: vase; green,
purple/red foliage; brown
fruit
Flower: showy; blue
Culture: full sun to shade; acid to alkaline
pH; medium salt tolerance; medium drought
tolerance; pest resistant

Notes: nice accent for interior landscapes or
for the garden
Uses: groundcover, mass planting, edging

Philodendron scandens (fill-loe-DEN-drun SCAN-denz)

Common name:
Heart-Leaf Philodendron
Zone: 10b-11
Size: 6" as a ground-
cover; moderate to fast
growth; 18 to 24" spacing
Form: spreading vine;
green foliage
Flower: not showy;
green
Culture: partial to full
shade; acid to slightly alkaline pH; medium
salt tolerance; medium drought tolerance; pest
resistant
Notes: commonly grown on a totem for

indoor use; also used as a groundcover in
malls
Uses: container, indoors, hanging basket,
cascade effect

Polyscias fruticosa (poe-LISS-see-us froo-tick-KOE-suh)

Common name:
Ming Aralia
Zone: 10a–11
Size: 4-6' tall; 3-5' wide;
slow growth; 24 to 36"
spacing
Form: round,
upright/erect; green,
dissected foliage
Flower: not showy;
creamy white

Culture: full sun to partial shade; tolerates occasional wet soil; acid to slightly alkaline pH; medium salt tolerance; high drought tolerance; pest sensitive
Notes: popular house-plant occasionally grown in the garden in south Florida; prefers bright light indoors
Uses: bonsai, container, specimen, foundation, border, accent, cut foliage, indoors

Sansevieria trifasciata

(san-sev-VEER-ree-uh try-fash-shee-AY-tuh)
Common name: Snake Plant,
Mother-in-Law's Tongue
Zone: 10-11
Size: 3-5' tall; 2-3' wide; slow growth; 18 to 24"
spacing
Form: upright/erect; green, variegated and
striped foliage; red fruit
Flower: showy; green, creamy-white
Culture: full sun to shade; acid to alkaline pH;
high salt tolerance; high drought tolerance; pest
resistant
Notes: dwarf cultivars and those with yellow
margins are popular; withstands long periods of
neglect; can be grown outdoors; becomes weedy
Uses: border, mass planting, specimen, container
or planter, naturalizing, indoors

Setcreasea pallida (SET-kree-zee-uh PAL-lid-duh)

Common name:
Purple Heart, Purple Queen

Zone: 9a-11

Size: 12-18" tall; variable spread; moderate growth; 18 to 24" spacing

Form: spreading; purple foliage

Flower: somewhat showy; pink

Culture: full sun to

partial shade; acid to alkaline pH; medium salt tolerance; high drought tolerance; pest resistant

Notes: purple foliage makes this a popular house-plant in a bright location; suited for outdoor use in south Florida

Uses: groundcover, container, mass planting, hanging basket, indoors, cascade effect

Spathiphyllum spp. (spath-ih-FILL-um species)

Common name:
Spathiphyllum, Peace Lily

Zone: 10a-11

Size: 18-24" tall and wide; moderate growth; 18 to 24" spacing

Form: upright; green foliage

Flower: showy; white, pink

Culture: shade; acid to

slightly alkaline pH; low salt tolerance; low drought tolerance; pest sensitive

Notes: popular house-plant; suited for outdoor use in south Florida in the shade

Uses: container, mass planting, indoors

Syngonium podophyllum (sin-GO-nee-um poe-doe-FILL-lum)

Common name:
Syngonium, Nephthytis
Zone: 10b-11
Size: variable height and spread; fast growth; 24 to 36" spacing
Form: spreading, prostrate (flat) vine; variegated, green foliage
Flower: not showy; creamy-white, green

Culture: partial to full shade; tolerates occasional wet soil; acid to slightly alkaline pH; low salt tolerance; medium drought tolerance; pest sensitive
Notes: climbs up trunks and totems; very weedy in south Florida
Uses: groundcover, mass planting, container, indoors, hanging basket, cascade effect

Zebrina pendula (zee-BRYE-nuh PEND-yoo-luh)

Common name:
Wandering Jew
Zone: 9a-11
Size: 6-12" tall; variable spread; fast growth; 18 to 24" spacing
Form: prostrate (flat), spreading; green, purple/red and silver, variegated foliage
Flower: not showy; pink

Culture: partial to full shade; tolerates occasional wet soil; acid to slightly alkaline pH; low salt tolerance; medium drought tolerance; pest resistant
Notes: makes a good house-plant in a sunny spot, can become a weed in the garden as they spread
Uses: mass planting, container, hanging basket, indoors, cascade effect

APPENDICES

Appendix 1.
Shade tolerant plants
TURF
St. Augustine Grass

BEDDING PLANTS
Flowering Tobacco**
Impatiens**
New Guinea Impatiens**

PERENNIALS
Butterfly Ginger
Caladium*
Jacobinia*
Variegated Shellflower

GROUND COVERS
Algerian Ivy*
Autumn Fern*
Boston Fern*
Cast Iron Plant*
English Ivy*
Holly Fern*
Lance Dracaena*
Lilyturf*
Mondo Grass
Oyster Plant

PALMS
Bamboo Palm*
Cabbage Palm
Lady Palm
Macarthur Palm
Microspadix Palm*
Sentry Palm
Solitaire Palm
Windmill Palm*

SHRUBS
Anise
Aralia
Azalea
Bigleaf Hydrangea*

Boxwood
Camellia
Cleyera
Crape Jasmine
Dwarf Schefflera
Fatsia*
Fortune's Mahonia*
Gardenia
Leather Fern*
Sandankwa Viburnum
Saw Palmetto
Selloum
Sweet Viburnum
Wild Coffee
'Xanadu' Philodendron

TREES
American Hornbeam
Flowering Dogwood
Fringe Tree
Japanese Maple
Podocarpus
Simpson's Stopper

FOLIAGE PLANTS
Aglaonema*
Corn plant*
Dracaena
Dumbcane*
Elephants Ear
Golden Pothos*
Heart-leaf Philodendron*
Ming Aralia
Painted Fingernail Plant
Prayer Plant*
Purple Heart
Reflexed Dracaena
Snake Plant
Spathiphyllum*
Syngonium*
Wandering Jew
* prefers shade or partial shade
** needs shade in summer

Appendix 2.
Salt tolerant plants
ANNUALS
Blue Daze
Blue Salvia*
Cherry Salvia*
Dianthus*
Gaillardia
Geranium
Marigold*
Periwinkle
Red Salvia*
Snapdragon*

FOLIAGE
Snake Plant

TURF
Bermuda Grass
St. Augustine Grass

GROUND COVERS
Asparagus Fern
Beach Sunflower
Dwarf Jasmine
Junipers
Lantanas
Liriope
Wedelia

PALMS
Cabbage Palm
Canary Island Date Palm
Coconut Palm
Date Palms
European Fan Palm
Florida Thatch Palm
Foxtail Palm
Jelly Palm
King Sago (not a true palm)
Latan Palm
Washingtonia Palm

PERENNIALS
Crinum Lily
Fakahatchee Grass
Pampas Grass

SHRUBS
Brush-cherry
Cape Honeysuckle

Century Plant
Cocoplum
Florida Privet
Indian Hawthorn
Japanese Privet
Leather Fern
Marlberry
Natal Plum
Oleander
Photinia
Pineapple Guava
Pittosporum
Round-leaf Hawthorn
Sandankwa Viburnum
Saw Palmetto
Scaevola
'Schellings Dwarf' Holly
Tropical Hibiscus
Wax Myrtle
Yellow Elder
Yucca

TREES
Arborvitae
Black Olive
Buttonwood
Frangipani
Geiger
Gumbo Limbo
Jerusalem Thorn
Leyland Cypress
Live Oak
Mahogany
Podocarpus
Santa Maria
Sea Grape
Simpson's Stopper
Slash Pine
Southern Magnolia
Southern Red Cedar
Sycamore
Wild Tamarind
* only fair salt tolerance

Appendix 3.
Large shrubs and small trees
SHRUBS
Anise
Brush-Cherry
Butterflybush
Camellia
Cleyera
Cocoplum
Dwarf Poinciana
Florida Privet
Japanese Privet
Marlberry
Orange Jasmine
Pineapple Guava
Powder Puff
Redtip Photinia
Rose-of-Sharon
Round-leaf Hawthorn
Surinam Cherry
Sweet Osmanthus
Sweet Viburnum
Tibouchina
Tropical Hibiscus
Wax Myrtle

SMALL TREES
Banana
Citrus
Crape Myrtle
Flowering Dogwood
Frangipani
Fringetree
Geiger Tree
Guava
Japanese Maple
Jerusalem Thorn
Loquat
Redbud
Saucer Magnolia
Silver Buttonwood
Simpson's Stopper
Spineless Yucca
Trumpet Tree
Weeping Bottlebrush

Appendix 4.
Plants tolerating wet soil
GROUND COVERS
Wedelia
SHRUBS
African Iris
Butterfly Ginger
Crinum Lily
Elephant Ear
Fakahatchee Grass
Florida Privet
Leather Fern
'Schellings Dwarf' Holly
Variegated Shell Ginger

PALMS
Cabbage Palm
Paurotis Palm

TREES
Bald Cypress
Banana
Green Ash
Pond Cypress
Red Maple
River Birch
Sycamore
Wax Myrtle

Appendix 5.
Plants with showy flowers
GROUND COVERS
Beach Sunflower
Carolina Yellow-Jasmine
Dwarf Gardenia
Gold Mound Lantana
Periwinkle
Society Garlic
Trailing Lantana
Wedelia

VINES
Allamanda
Bengal Clock Vine
Confederate Jasmine
Flame Vine
Mandevilla
Passion Vine

SHRUBS

African Bush Daisy
Azalea
Bigleaf Hydrangea
Bougainvillea
Bush Allamanda
Bush Clock Vine
Butterfly-Bush
Camellia
Candlebush
Cape Honeysuckle
Chenille Plant
Downy Jasmine
Dwarf Oleander
Dwarf Poinciana
Fatsia
Firebush
Firecracker Plant
Gardenia
Glossy Abelia
Indian Hawthorn
Ixora
Japanese Ligustrum
Nandina
Pinwheel Jasmine
Plumbago
Powder Puff
Redtip Photinia
Rose-of-Sharon
Roundleaf Hawthorn
Spanish Dagger
Spiraea
Tibouchina
Tropical Hibiscus
Thryallis
Yellow Elder

TREES

'Bradford' Callery Pear
Crape Myrtle
Eastern Redbud
Flamegold
Flowering Dogwood
Frangipani
Fringetree
Geiger-Tree
Golden-Shower
Jacaranda
Jerusalem Thorn
Pongam
Royal Poinciana
Saucer Magnolia
Simpson's Stopper
Southern Magnolia
Spineless Yucca
Trumpet Tree
Weeping Bottlebrush
White Bird-of-Paradise

Appendix 6.
Plants suited for indoor use not listed in the foliage section

Ground covers: Asparagus Fern, Boston Fern, Cast Iron Plant, Holly Fern, Ivy, Impatiens, Lilyturf, Mondo Grass and Silver Vase.

Palms: Areca Palm, Bamboo Palm, Chinese Fan Palm, Christmas Palm, Fishtail Palm, and Kentia Palm.

Shrubs: Aralia, Croton, Dwarf Schefflera, Fatsia and Selloum.

Trees: Black Olive (especially 'Shady Lady'), Cuban Laurel, Fiddle Leaf Fig, Norfolk Island Pine, Rubber Tree, Schefflera, Spineless Yucca and Weeping Fig.

INDEX